FLASHBACKS

Corporal Michael Willey

Copyright © 2016 Michael Willey

The rights of Michael Willey to be identified as the authors of this work
has been asserted by him in accordance with the
Copyright, Designs and Patents Act 1988.

ISBN: 978-1-910719-16-9

All rights reserved. No part of this publication may be reproduced
or transmitted in any form or by any means, electronic or mechanical.
Including photocopying, recording, or any information storage and retrieval
system without permission in writing from the author.

Published for Michael Willey by
Verité CM Limited,
Unit 2, Martlets Way, Goring Business Park,
Goring-by-Sea, West Sussex BN12 4HF

+44 (0) 1903 241975
email: enquiries@veritecm.com
Web: www.veritecm.com

British Library Cataloguing Data

A catalogue record of this book is available from The British Library

Design and Typesetting by Verité CM Ltd

Printed in England

DEDICATION

This book is mainly dedicated to my good friend and brother in arms Private John. The infantryman I spent many months with in hospital as we tried to support each other through PTSD.

It is also dedicated to the people listed as my friends, those people who were there for me when the government let me down. The same way they have let down so many physically and mentally wounded servicemen. The fact remains, just over two hundred and fifty servicemen died in action during the Falklands war, There has been more servicemen and women who have committed suicide since the Falklands, than died in that action. The only thing that has changed over the last thirty years, there are more suicides and servicemen suffering with PTSD, than there are dying in action. The troubles in Northern Ireland lasted years along with the other conflicts, like Bosnia. Afghanistan and although a lot of those conflicts are finished, they are still claiming the lives of British servicemen. You can mend a bullet wound, you can see a bullet wound, you cannot see or mend so easily a broken mind and the truth is that I was fortunate to spend many months in a military hospital surrounded by military staff. Also the people I named as being there for me, through their care of me, gave me the strength to fight on. Those people and a promise I made to my uncle to return his sister to Greece, only achieved by the intervention of Her Majesty The Queen, for which I will be eternally grateful.

Her action proved that I was right to serve the Queen, even if we feel let down by the country. The armed forces are all members of a unique family, the largest family in Great Britain and every member swears allegiance to the Queen. Being a member of that family gives you courage, dedication to duty and above all else loyalty. Loyalty is a doubled edged sword and although this book is my story of post-traumatic stress disorder. It also tells a story of loyalty, the loyalty of Her Majesty The Queen to a mere corporal, she intervened to help me when I was first medically discharged from the military. The loyalty of the Royal family to their servicemen has never come in to question and is now in the capable hands of Prince William and Prince Harry. Due to my poor mental state at the time, I sent a copy of this book to Prince William, asking for his help in publishing my story. Prince William wrote back to me, congratulating me in writing the book. In his letter he rightly informed me, he could not show favouritism to one ex-servicemen when so many were suffering. I know that was the right decision as I was at the time suffering a great deal with flashbacks. His letter was still one of loyalty to an ex serviceman and a fellow brother in arms. That letter in the same way as the letter I received from HM The Queen some twenty five years ago, help to save my life at a time I was suffering a great deal.

THANKS

To enable me to still be alive today, I have to thank in order of their appearance in my life the following people. The people listed below, showed me love, compassion or were there for me at the most crucial times in my life, since leaving the army.

RAY BROWN
PHYLLIS ELIZABETH JONES
CAROLE ANNE GWINNELL
PAUL AND MAUREEN MARKS
THE Queen
I remain Ma'am your obedient servant.
LES ELLIOT
MICHAEL AND SONIA PHILLIPOU
THE KIOUSI FAMILY IN GREECE
THE GIOPPATTO FAMILY IN ITALY
TERRY AND JENNIFER STRAW
THE PEOPLE OF DINNINGTON
MY WIFE AND CHILDREN
PAUL AND MICHELLE BEECH
THE BRITISH LEGION
PRINCE WILLIAM
RAY DICKINSON

FLASHBACKS

Post-traumatic Stress Disorder. That's what they are telling me, known as PTSD. I, like many soldiers have changed the letters to what it should be known as, that is *Pick The Suicide Day* as I know it is coming to me, like so many of my friends and colleagues it has already claimed. I am just not sure when I will kill myself, or even more frightening someone else, before it takes me. The one thing that makes you realise you have got it, is your uncontrollable mind, the thoughts of injustice and cruelty which you seem to carry around as a soldier, those same thoughts that become a reality as a wounded man with PTSD.

I know I am nearly thirty years old and I am sat outside the shrink's (psychiatrist's) office in a military hospital somewhere in London. I am a Corporal and I have been places and done things, yet I don't know how I got here. I know I am drugged up. I know that because I have to report every day to take my pills in front of the Royal Air Force medic. I did remember getting injured and having plastic surgery, mainly on my face, but that was a couple of years ago. I remember it as that was my first visit to a military hospital. So how did that get me to being sat outside a psychiatrist's office? I saw *'One Flew over the Cuckoo's Nest'* and now I was in it. I was then brought into what was to become my real world for the most of my life.

I heard a raised voice and the sound of a crash, which sounded like something being thrown through a window,

FLASHBACKS

it was a table thrown by Rifleman T. He was trying to explain to the civilian psychiatrist why he was angry. He had been allowed out on weekend leave from the hospital. His voice full of anger was telling the shrink how he had ended up being brought back into the hospital by the Military Police. He had decided like so many of us soldiers that the way to deal with his nightmares was to get drunk. Getting drunk along with the medication was a time bomb, just waiting to explode.

He was screaming at the shrink, 'You haven't got a clue what's happening in my head.'

He was telling the shrink about that night out. He was saying how he had been out a couple of hours and whilst he was enjoying his drink, he noticed a man had looked at him and was laughing. Of course the poor guy was probably having a laugh with his mates and unfortunately happened to be looking the way of the rifleman. Whatever the guy was laughing about did not come in to the equation, as far as the rifleman was concerned, the laughing man was being disrespectful. The rifleman was thinking of his two mates blown to bits, whilst on a patrol, so he somehow connected the laughing man. Although he couldn't explain why he had picked up a chair in the pub and ran across to smash it over the poor guy's head, he said he did it because he was angry.

Hence the crash that I had just heard was indeed the chair that Rifleman T was sat on; he had decided to throw the chair through the glass window. That explained the noise and where the crash had come from, he had thrown it because the shrink was not showing him any compassion or understanding, Rifleman T believed he was wasting his time and the shrink didn't have a clue what he was talking about. Within a few seconds of the crash, the door opened and an angered Rifleman T was running out, telling me in passing, 'You are wasting your fucking time Corporal.' I didn't understand that until the shrink came to the door, stood at the side of me and said to poor Rifleman T, who was by then in bits on the floor. 'Would you like to come and talk about your problems?'

I could not help myself, I burst into laughter as I could not believe that this shrink appeared not to realise what I then realised, having heard Rifleman T pouring his heart out. I knew I had the same anger built up inside me. This was serious, I thought, I am seriously messed up here, I don't know how I got here and I am being assessed and treated by a civilian shrink who at a guess was around my age. How the hell can a civilian who has studied the mind on paper ever understand what happens to real soldiers who get mentally messed up.

My appointment with the shrink was then cancelled and I was told to go back to my ward. I still didn't realise why I was there, as I had no recollection of doing anything wrong at the time. Meanwhile Rifleman T was given an injection to apparently calm him down. Like a good soldier I went back to the ward and looked around at the guys that were in with me, mainly infantrymen, a marine and me. There were a couple of Lance Corporals and around six Privates, being a military hospital. I was put in charge of the servicemen in our part of the ward, me having the highest rank. It didn't need much discipline as nearly everyone was on some sort of medication and when anyone decided they wanted to wake up and kick off, they were instantly restrained and then sedated with more drugs.

FLASHBACKS

I remember that night in hospital, maybe it was because of the trauma I had witnessed that day with rifleman T, or it could have been the thoughts of my own situation. Whatever the reason didn't matter, what mattered was that night, as that was to become the night that my flashbacks began. My first flashback was not of a military nature as such, more of a civilian problem with my twin brother. It seemed to start as soon as I closed my eyes to go to sleep. I drifted off and it seemed almost immediate that my mind took me back to being twenty years old. I started dreaming about the time I had been on a promotion course in North Yorkshire, Catterick Garrison to be exact. I had gone home on leave for the weekend, but I failed to return to camp. I remembered I had gone home on the Friday and met up with my sister. She told me that my twin brother Graham had tried to kill himself and that I could find him in a mental hospital in Sheffield. I knew the hospital as it was famous around Rotherham and Sheffield. If you did something stupid in those days, people would say you are going to end up in Middlewood. My sister said, she had been to see Graham, but she did not know what was wrong with him. She could only say that a doctor had diagnosed something called schizophrenia. She didn't know what it was and I didn't have a clue either, I just knew he needed me.

I got to the hospital and found out where he was being kept, I explained to a nurse on his ward that I was a soldier on week-end leave and as I had very little time, could I be allowed to see my twin. She took me to his room and Graham was in a padded room with bars on the window, a bed and a blanket. I asked him if he was okay and he just mumbled get me out of

FLASHBACKS

here Mick. I explained to him, it may be difficult as apparently he had been taken there by the police. I asked him why he wanted to take his own life. He said something about being afraid as he had been to sea. He wasn't making sense at the time, he kept saying they were electrocuting him and pleading with me to get him out. My flashback then took me to the dark place that could have been one of the reasons Graham wanted to kill himself. We were seven years old and had been awakened one night with the sounds of men shouting and arguing. At that time Graham and I slept in the same bed at the side of the window. We both sat up and looked out of the window at the same time. We saw one of our mother's lovers, in the back garden of our terraced house. His name was Tony, a Polish immigrant who had settled in England after the Second World War. He had turned up drunk and was shouting at the back door, "come out you bastard". He was referring to the man who had replaced him in our mother's life as he and my mother had had a fall out. That night Tony had decided he wanted to kill the man who had replaced him in our mother's life. That man's name was Leo and he and Tony used to be friends. We could hear my mother telling Leo not to open the door, unfortunately for Leo he did not listen to our mother. He ran out into the back yard and started to rant at Tony. Graham and I just watched as Tony rammed a breadknife into Leo's stomach several times until Leo collapsed and his body became still on the floor. He never moved again, the blood reflected in the moonlight, like an oil slick covering the whole of the back yard. We watched as Tony dropped the knife on the floor and ran off. That would be the last time we would see Tony,

FLASHBACKS

it would also be the last time my mother had any time with Tony. He was sentenced to seven years in Wakefield Prison for the manslaughter. He sent hundreds of letters to my mother begging her to visit and after several months of not being visited by our mother, Tony hung himself in his cell.

You would think that seeing Tony killed would be the reason for my flashback. The real reason for my flashback was because I was remembering my twin in the mental hospital in Sheffield. Now it appeared I was in a similar position, the only difference being I was trapped in a military hospital. Having just heard the rifleman pouring his heart out, I thought of my twin begging me to stop them, he was begging me to get him out of there. I lost track of time that weekend with Graham and even though my weekend pass was up, I couldn't leave my twin. It was 1973 and my twin was having a specialist treatment, called electric shock treatment. The doctors told me it was for his own good and that it would stop him having the evil bad thoughts that were in his mind... yet my twin was pleading with me to stop them. At that time I believed what the doctor was telling me, as such I failed to get my brother out of there and just waited for him to come back from his treatment. He never came back again as the twin I had grown up with. Even to this day I knew what they did to him was barbaric and I have never stopped feeling guilty for letting them do it. I gave myself up to the army after spending a few days with my twin. Fortunately for me, my Commanding Officer at that time had knowledge of schizophrenia, having a brother himself with the disease. Rather than ruining my army career, I was allowed to finish my course and get promoted. The staff at the hospital confirmed that I had spent the days absent without leave with my twin brother.

With those memories, my mind returned to the predicament I found myself in after that flashback, I knew from the experience with my twin that I was not in a good place, but thought to myself; until I find out what has happened to me I will go along with the system. Just in case I had schizophrenia without knowing it.

The next few days seem to pass quite quickly and I was actually thinking to myself whatever was wrong with me wasn't too bad, I had managed to chat me up an RAF nurse, who worked on another ward, she was in charge of the wives of serviceman, some having babies, others hysterectomies. Being wives of servicemen they were also entitled to be treated by the military personnel in a military hospital. She had no idea I was a patient from another ward and as I was in civilian clothes at the time, I believe she thought I was a visitor to one of her patients.

All was going quite well, I would just sneak off my ward and wander the massive hospital. There were no mobile phones then and being a bit of a communications expert, I had no problem getting into a sister's office and finding myself a phone, I could use the phone to contack a girlfriend I had at home in Rotherham.

It was quite easy to sneak off the ward and go walk about as the night nurses were mainly male, they were kept busy at night, dishing out medicine. I would just take my medicine, return to my bed, stuff the pillow under the sheets, as if I were in bed and take off, wandering the hospital to find an office with

FLASHBACKS

a phone. I managed to find a ward with an empty office and a phone. I sat down and proceeded to phone the girlfriend I had in Rotherham. I had been on the phone about forty minutes, when the office door sprung open and in walked two female officers, a Major and a Captain who were members of the Queen Alexander's Royal Army Nursing Corps, known as QARANCs. My immediate thoughts were that I was in big trouble, I looked up at them and was about to speak when the major looked me straight in the face, smiled and said sorry doctor, we will come back later.' I acknowledged them, without saying a word. I just smiled back and gave them a wave as they departed. I assumed they would be off to check out the new doctor, I waited two minutes and did a runner back to my ward.

All was okay until I decided to push my luck a few days later and I was on the phone in that same office. The office door opened again, this time it was the same major, accompanied by one of the corporals off my ward. He had seen seen me leave the ward and decided to followed me. I sarcastically saluted the Major and was escorted back to my ward. Whatever was wrong with me had given me a 'don't give a shit about anything' attitude.

Being a military hospital, I was charged under section sixty nine of the Queen's regulations, in that contrary to good order and military discipline, I took the law into my own hands by finding the phone to use without having consent. I could not think what to tell the commanding officer as I was a little stuck for words, I ended up telling him, I was behaving that way because no one was telling me how I had ended up in hospital, I had used the phone as I just wanted to speak to someone who may be able to help me find out what was wrong with me. I went on to tell him that before I came into hospital, I had been seeing a girlfriend in Rotherham. He went on to ask me what she had told me. I said she had told me that she had met me over a year ago and at that time I was on leave from the same military hospital, having had plastic surgery on my face for an injury. She said as far as she knew, I had left the hospital and had returned to Catterick, where she believed I was an instructor, training potential officers. Apparently I had not been in touch with her for a few months and she had assumed that I had finished with her.

After my explanation, I was not given any punishment for my use of the phone or for wandering off the ward. Indirectly I was punished as that night I went for my medication as normal and I found myself on a larger dose of pills. I remembered going from two to three tablets and starting to feel tired. Having been in the hospital for what seemed like weeks, without any access to the outside world I was starting to feel isolated and angry. The anger became more disruptive, I didn't know why I was angry, I just knew I was and I wanted to escape it. It was around that time that I had my first thoughts of suicide. Why had I never thought of suicide until now, God only knows. I only knew I did not know what was wrong with me. I then refused to do anything I was told, I told the medical staff I wanted to go back to my unit and I would not be held responsible for my actions if I was not released.

That turned out to be a bad move on my part, I was told I had to show them that I was okay before I would be allowed to leave hospital or even go on leave. With those words I felt

FLASHBACKS

threatened and angry, I decided that they would not stop me leaving and went on to trash the ward. My rage lasted a couple of minutes and the last thing I remembered was being restrained and the prick in my arm, as they sent me off to sleep.

Two months had passed by then and I got a visit from one of my mates from camp. He told me he was only allowed to see me for a few minutes as I was apparently very ill and he was not to discuss what had happened to me, to put me in hospital.

Of course in the army a mate would never hold that sort of information back from another mate, especially soldiers that had joined up together. He told me I had been injured over a year ago and that at that time I had spent a few months in hospital. He knew after I left hospital I had been sent on a mountain leadership course in Scotland, some place near Fort William. I had stayed in Scotland after that course and went straight onto another course, to also become a canoeing instructor. I told him I remembered what he was telling me about the courses as I remembered climbing Ben Nevis and some students who were walking up the long slope to get to the top of mountain, at the same time as we were climbing. They were shouting across, you are all going to die, which to us was quite funny. I did remember shitting myself as we got higher and higher, to the point of no return, I went on to tell my mate how I told the parachute regiment sergeant instructor that those students may be right. The sergeant just came straight back at me with, airborne mate. I said thanks sergeant but that is something I don't want to be at the moment.

My mate then went on to tell me that after I had finished the courses, I was posted to recruit training, somewhere near

FLASHBACKS

Newcastle. I remembered that as well as that was where I was stationed when I got divorced. He said you may have not been well there mate as apparently you smacked a recruit and had a run in with his troop commander, some officer. The commanding officer didn't deem that you were at fault with the recruit as apparently he had been pushing his weight around and you were defending another recruit. His troop officer also was given a bollocking as he was told he should not have brought you in front of the commanding officer. As you had done all the courses to become a training instructor you were sent from Newcastle to Catterick and that was your last job, training potential officers.

I had apparently been at Catterick about six months when I supposedly went crazy, attacking an officer, whilst on a training exercise. As far as he was aware, I had attacked the officer because he had said something wrong to me.

I don't know what scared me most, thinking I could have been thrown in jail and demoted, for attacking an officer or the fact that I was in a military hospital because I had lost the plot. I then started to realise that my mind wasn't right, I did not know how to stop the anger and it appeared my self-destruct button was getting the better of me.

I thanked my mate for telling me everything and I started to conform a bit more as I saw soldiers being allowed out on leave, even Rifleman T, if they behaved and took their medicine like good zombies. I knew I was having suicidal thoughts at the time, but I also thought I would like to go and see my family before I kill myself. I knew whatever had happened to me, I wanted to see my mother and my brothers and sister.

FLASHBACKS

I had managed to behave for a week, mainly because I was by then on five tablets a day and spent most of my time in a daze just going through the motions. I also had been adopted by a young private, who had only seen action once and ended up in hospital, having had some sort of breakdown. I became a bit of a hero of his, me being a corporal and him not being long out of training. He couldn't believe that I would call him John and be nice to him. As I was a corporal he believed he had to kiss my ass. I grew attached to John, as I had told him about all the courses I had done, from skiing, canoeing, free fall parachuting to mountaineering, I shared with him some of my tours of duty in the more exotic places in the world I had been with the army. He became a good mate, he told me about why he joined the army. His parents had left him when he was a few years old and he had been brought up by his grandmother. I knew his background would be like that of so many soldiers. The tougher the regiment, the more tragic the childhood, was the way I saw things.

Talking to John reminded me of when I was fifteen and I first went to join the army. I had had a very tough childhood and I saw the army as an escape. My mother was Greek and we had left my father before I was six, so you can imagine childhood was rough to say the least. I did gain something from it that I wouldn't have gained from a normal childhood and that was the ability to live on my wits. That ability was already present at fifteen, which was lucky as I needed all my wits about me when it came time to enlist in the army. Basically at fifteen, your parents or guardian have to sign the enlistment papers, for you to join the army as a boy soldier. My mother being Greek did not realise she had to sign me into the army. Maybe it was because when she was fifteen, she was fighting Germans and she thought I could join without her permission.

I remember the day I enlisted, two sergeants arrived at our two bedroom terraced house. We had lived there several years, my mother with the lover of the day in one bedroom and us six children in the other. Up to that point I had not realised that the army sent soldiers to your home with the enlistment papers. I thought they would just give them me to take home after I had visited the careers office. I got that part wrong as that day, there they were, knocking at the back door; luckily I was home and let them in. My mother was in bed, I told the two sergeants my mother was ill and that she was in the bath, trying to sweat out the illness. That itself would have been a miracle as we did not have a bathroom, but they did not know that. I said I could take the papers up to her to sign if that's alright as she had only just gone in the bath. They said that they were supposed to see her sign them, but under the circumstances it would be alright. If she could just shout down it is okay after she signs the papers. They gave me a pen and I went upstairs. I opened the bedroom door, my mother had her back to me, so I signed the paper with her signature, I then shook my mother and said, 'The coalman, has delivered some coal across the road and the man said he will give me half a crown to shovel it down his cellar for him.' I told my mother the man was at the bottom of the steps and if she could just shout it's okay for me to go, I would give her the money I earned. My mother shouted, 'It is okay love he can go, just make sure you pay him,' she shouted louder. I ran down the stairs and explained to the soldiers that

FLASHBACKS

my mother was Greek and they don't get paid in the Greek army, both men laughed and left.

I remembered that feeling of freedom from the tragedy of my childhood. The Army must be better than the future I could look forward to as a fifteen year old boy from Rotherham. At the time it was either the steelworks or the pit and having spent a lot of my time as a small boy thrown in a cellar full of coal I realised I did not like the dark, or the dirt. That was how Graham and I ended up working together in the steel works. Our job there was to cut up steel sections and when we got a little bigger, we would then be allowed to work on pushing steel billets through rollers. The only thing you had to look forward too was getting bigger and stronger, that would enable you to lift bigger billets and earn more money. It also gave you a chance of dying as there were quite a few deaths in the steel works in those days. I was not afraid of death, I was more afraid of catching the red hot billets as they came through the rollers. I had witnessed someone getting burned as the red hot billet sliced through the side of his leg as he was not concentrating. I had already dealt with violent death as a seven year old and at ten I remembered me and my twin brother having to lift the corpse of a crazy old man. He was about seventy five years old and lived in our cellar. We knew him as Ralph, a punch drunk boxer who was obviously mentally ill. He lived in our cellar and our mother would feed him now and again. As the cellar grates had been bricked up, there was no natural light that could get in to the cellar and as such you never knew what time of day it was. My mother used this to her advantage, if she had no food to feed Ralph. It may be blue skies and sunshine outside and midday, Ralph would shout up, 'Vasso where is my dinner?' If my Mother had no food she would just shout. 'Go back to bed you crazy old man, it's midnight.'

Of course on Friday when it was time to get his dole money, my mother would wake him with breakfast and send him off to collect his money to pay her. We all laughed about that, until he died of course. Graham and I as ten year olds had to carry his corpse up two flights of stairs and drop him on a bed, before my mother contacked the authorities. It would not have looked very good for her had they found Ralph where he died. Instead they found our dead lodger in a nice clean bed.

My mother never found out about how she had unwillingly got me in the army. If I had had a good childhood maybe I would have thought twice about becoming a soldier, but the truth was the only chance I had in life as far as I was concerned, was to join the army. You could also say it was in my blood as although I never really knew my father I knew that he met my mother during the war in Greece. At that time he was twenty one and had been in the army since the beginning of the war. He had enlisted in to the 17/21st Lancers, the motto of which was 'death or glory.' Of course as soldiers, you see both, you realise there is no glory in death and to be given a medal to justify killing someone, who is just doing his job the same as you, never sat well in my mind..

Although we left my father when I was five, I still remember all the death or glory he dished out to us all. How he would always be drunk and firstly abuse us kids, then our mother. I say kids because there were six of us, five boys and the youngest, still in the cot when we left my father, was our sister.

The abuse was mainly mental abuse as he would use us kids as a tool to get the attention from our mother. He did, however, tell us stories about being a soldier when he was drunk, he told us about being in the Lancers; how he had to fight through Italy before he got to Greece. He told us about Monte Casino and how that was the worst part of the war for him, he told us how lots of his friends died there.

I understand him now I am stuck in a hospital with lots of soldiers who are mentally messed up. Of course then I didn't have a clue. I only remember him being drunk most of the time and picking on my twin brother.

I remembered a particular time, when Graham and I were just five years old. Graham had a bit of a speech impediment, I believe it came out of the fear of being constantly thrown down the cellar and left in the dark. Sadly at that time, Graham being thrown in the cellar was our father's favourite punishment. Graham never learned as I did to avoid our father when he came in pissed, he would always go up to him for attention. You would have thought that our father would have been more loving towards his twins as we were the only two out of the six children that looked English. All the others looked Greek, dark hair, brown eyes and a tanned complexion.

Graham and I were English looking, red rosy cheeks and blue eyes. I apparently looked like my father when he was a child. That aside, my father came in drunk as usual, Graham, as usual went up to him and asked if he could have a grint of water. My father slapped him across the face and shouted at him

FLASHBACKS

to say drink of water, 'Now ask properly,' he told my twin. Graham once again asked for a grint of water. My father picked him up by his arm, his body totally off the ground, opened what was the door to the cellar and threw Graham downstairs into the dark, which he knew Graham hated. I grabbed my dad's arm to make him let go of Graham and of course, I ended up down the cellar with Graham. Luckily it was summer and it was still quite light outside as we could see the light through the grate. I got Graham to follow me, and we crawled over the coal that had been delivered that day and climbed up through the grate outside to freedom. Graham was in total fear of getting caught, I personally didn't care less and I only had plans to escape.

We made our escape, only to be seen by my father's mother, our grandmother. She lived a few doors down from us on the terraced road we lived on, she would watch out for us when she could. She knocked on the door and after a while our dad came to the door, pulling his trousers up. It was quite obvious that he had just been having his way with our mother. I don't think it was something my mother wanted to do, but I believe she gave in to him to protect us, as she did on many occasions. It wasn't until that night that I realised why my dad, threw us in to the cellar, it was so he could have his way with our mother. That night our two elder brothers were in bed, our smallest brother, who was also in bed, being only two he knew nothing, that left our sister, asleep in our cot. As such, it was always either Graham or me that ruined his seduction plans.

I remember that night, as it was to become a changing point in our lives as children, as that was the night we left our father.

FLASHBACKS

As usual he had thrown me and Graham back in the cellar, whilst being held back by our mother. At the same time he was punching our mother as she tried to stop this mad man from abusing us. She managed to stop him getting me and Graham into the cellar and she told us to run upstairs to bed, which is what we did. I could hear my mother being punched and beaten, something she never got used to, even when he beat her and she fell down the stairs, losing a baby, something she told us later.

Anyway that night seemed to be dragging on forever. I could hear the constant screaming and fighting. I crept down the stairs, the living room door was slightly ajar so I could see my mother and father shouting and fighting. I didn't understand why, I only knew my father was very jealous of my mother as she was very pretty.

Sadly my mother only married my father as she lost most of her family at the latter end of the war. She was seventeen in 1944 and by then she was in the resistance, fighting the Germans in the mountains of the Peloponnese, which made her a Spartan. She met my father when they were thrown together in Greece during the war. I don't know if they would have got together in any other way, I now know that they were two people damaged by the war.

Back to that night, I had crept down the stairs and was watching the war of my parents through the crack in between the door and the door frame, as the door was slightly ajar. The living room was also my parents' bedroom and as such there was a big double bed in the centre of the room.

FLASHBACKS

My father punched my mother in the face and I saw him go to kick her, I pushed open the door and told him to leave her alone. My mother grabbed his leg as he made a run to get me. My mother shouted, 'run Mickey.' I didn't run as I was frozen to the spot in fear. My father lifted me like a rag doll into the air, with his hand under my throat and pressed me against the door. At the same time I was trying to scream, I felt my father's grip on my throat just let go. I fell to the floor as my father fell at the same time on to the bed at the side of him.

One of the only things my mother had brought from Greece was a solid brass cigarette case that was about a foot long and weighed about three pounds. Ironically it was a wedding present, my mother had picked it up and caved it as hard as she could into my father's head. I was sure he was dead as he was flat down on the bed and blood was gushing everywhere.

My mother said, 'Quickly Mickey, go and wake up all your brothers and tell them to get dressed.' I did as I was told and I saw my mother leave through the front door. I thought – I hope she is not doing a runner and I am going to carry the can. Well as much as I could carry the can as a five year old, I just thought I was in trouble.

My mother said reassuringly, 'Don't worry Mickey we are going somewhere safe.' She said she was just going to the phone box to make a phone call. I thought she was going to phone an ambulance. My grandmother, my father's mother then appeared at the door and saw what had happened to her son.

She started screaming, 'Am going to fetch the police,' at which point my mother returned and told her in no uncertain terms where she should go. My father's mother treated my mother much the same way as her son. She made it quite clear my mother was a foreigner and was not accepted as a daughter-in-law. So my mother was really on her own trying to save her children, as we were all that she had in her life at that time.

With all those thoughts of my childhood, the flashback or nightmare comes to an end and I woke to find myself covered in sweat and staring out of the window at the side of my bed.

My mind slowly returns to my reality and I start to wonder if my childhood could be the reason I ended up in the military hospital? I knew it wasn't the reason, as I believed I had dealt with that part of my life, prior to joining the army. Although my childhood comes into my life a great deal, I knew the reason for my being in that hospital was something more devastating.

I started to think about when I had joined the army, at fifteen years old, fifteen and a half to be exact. I arrived at an army apprentice college in Yorkshire to join the Royal Signals. I was going to train to be a radio operator. Basically I was going to be a signaller, but had to get through two years of being a boy soldier to make sure I was brainwashed enough to do my duty.

Being the army they have to take your character down to rock bottom, this ensures what they get after training is a disciplined soldier. It must be that way, so when it comes to the crunch you have the training to deal with whatever you are faced with. Of course for my part I had been through a war with my childhood so the army could not really do anything to me. I was happy to get three meals a day and sheets on a bed.

The one saving grace throughout my life has been my sense of humour in the face of adversity, I always laughed or made people laugh, which again was something I had developed over the years for protection.

There were around six hundred young boys at the college, we would always parade in the morning and get inspected by the Regimental Sergeant Major, a fearsome tall Irish Guardsman.

The college was split into four squadrons that consisted of around one hundred and fifty boys. Each squadron had a couple of regular sergeants, who were mainly on their last few years in the army. My troop sergeant was a Coldstream Guardsman, who had been in the army around fifteen years. Later on I learned that we call the Guardsmen wooden tops. His name was Tom B. I could tell you what the B stood for, but you can guess. I thought he had took a dislike to me as he seemed to single me out after the first day we met.

We were stood outside the squadron office on parade, being told what we would be doing during our first three months of recruit training. Mainly the fact was we would not be allowed our civilian clothes for three months and if we were good and managed to get through the first three months our lives would improve as and when we got into one of the main squadrons. We then would be replaced by the new batch of recruits, as there were three intakes a year, with three breaks in between intakes.

Well Sergeant B came marching up and down in front of us, twisting his pace stick around as he marched. I had to admit I liked him as he was what I believed I wanted to be. He stopped in front of me, pushed the stick against my chest and asked me my name.

'Willey,' I said.

FLASHBACKS

'Not your first fucking name son,' was the reply.

I said, 'That is my surname.'

'In that case,' he said, 'if your name is Willey I am going to call you prick".

I did take slight offence at his comments, so when he pushed his drill stick up my nostril and said, 'Do you know what I have got at the end of this stick prick?'

I said, 'No sergeant.'

He said, 'A piece of fucking shit.'

I immediately replied with, 'Yes, it's on your side Sergeant.'

He quickly looked around at everyone laughing, looked over his shoulder to see if he could see anyone in the squadron office then punched me in the stomach causing me to curl up. Then he said, 'Anyone else care to be a comedian?'

I liked him because he came over later and said he liked me.

'I like a man with balls,' he said, 'you're funny but you got balls son.'

No one had ever spoken to me about having courage, as a child I had always believed I didn't have any courage, as I had always felt afraid. To say I had just had a good punch in the stomach, I seemed quite quite happy at the time. The sergeant had just physically abused me, said he liked me, told me I had got balls and I just took it.

Over that three months recruit training, he managed to get me thrown in and out of jail many times, and jankers, which basically meant me being made to parade in my best uniform at midnight and peeling potatoes in the kitchen or anything menial that would break my spirit. I was a good soldier I kept

FLASHBACKS

being told, but I needed to keep my mouth shut. I guess every time I felt I was being put down I would rebel as I was never going to allow anyone to abuse me, as I had had enough of that as a child and that was the whole reason I joined the army.

One of the ways of bringing you down to being subservient was to best you on parade. At that particular college, they had a massive parade square, at the front of which was a large flagpole. Sergeant B told us we have to imagine that the flag pole is a statue of Queen Victoria. Once a week they would have RSMs parade. Basically the RSM would walk up and down the new recruits for about half an hour, pretending to inspect the recruits in each squadron, with the normal boys soldiers in the back ground as they had all passed through the initial recruit training. Altogether there would be around six hundred boys on parade. The RSM just walks up and down tapping a recruit on the shoulder. He would just say, 'Boots,' or 'trousers' or 'kit.' It didn't matter what he said, when you were tapped on the shoulder the troop sergeant would

Three churbes and parade square. Army Apprentice College, Harrogate

FLASHBACKS

take your name and you would be on show parade, meaning that you had to prepare your smart uniform and report to the guard house at midnight, so the guard commander could tell you to go to bed. The guard commander very rarely inspected any of the poor sods on show parade, he would just send them to bed, reporting was just part of the game.

As it was difficult for the sergeants to write every recruit's name down that the RSM had tapped on parade, the tapped recruit would have to march around one hundred yards to the flagpole or statue of Queen Victoria as it was known and shout out. I am sorry my boots are dirty ma'am, or whatever the RSM had told them.

So you had lots of recruits marching up and down shouting, 'I am sorry Ma'am.'

All the thoughts of recruit training were going through my mind as I lay in my hospital bed.

I was smiling, thinking about one particular day at the army apprentice college. I remembered being on parade and the regimental sergeant major picking me out for my dirty boots. I remembered how I marched over to Queen Victoria and shouted I was sorry for having dirty boots. At which point, you are supposed to about turn and return to the spot where you were on parade and await the parade being dismissed. Of course I did not about turn or go back to my place in the parade. Instead I turned right and started to march towards the squadron accommodation block.

The Regimental Sergeant Major spotted me and shouted as only a RSM could shout, 'Where the hell do you think you are going?'

FLASHBACKS

I stopped and shouted back, 'Sir, I told Queen Victoria about my boots and she said I had to go and clean them straight away.'

The whole six hundred boys and the troop sergeants burst into hysterics. Unfortunately, the RSM was not as amused and shouted at two soldiers, 'Grab that man and throw him in jail.' At which point I was grabbed under each arm by two regimental policemen. They were running forward, as I was being dragged backwards on my heels, creating sparks from the segs fitted to the heels of my leather boots. They dragged me all the way to the guardroom, with the parade still in fits of laughter and the RSM trying to bring back the parade to a more military nature, than the hysterical mob I had created.

The last thing I heard was the RSM shouting, 'As you all think, that young man was funny you can all parade tomorrow morning at six a.m., that next day being Saturday. No one was to be allowed out of camp. It was still worth it to me, as I became famous for the first time in my life.

I was put in the guardroom, I wasn't locked up, just told to sit down and await my doom. I was sent for by the RSM straight after he had dismissed the parade. He asked me, if I found the army a joke and asked me why I had joined in the first place. I told him I wanted to escape my childhood and I didn't know any other way. He said fair enough son but if you want to stay in the army, he would have to see a vast improvement in my discipline.

'Yes sir,' I said. He then put me on show parade for two weeks, meaning every day, during the day, I did my army training, then in the evenings I would do chores, after which I would then have to parade at midnight. The one thing that did happen after that incident, I got loads of mates as everyone wanted to be my mate. I think it was because I did what they wanted to do, but were too afraid. That aside I ended up with the guy who is still my best friend to this day, a man called Ray Brown from Bradford.

Like waking up from a dream, reality kicked in once again as I realise I am in the hospital. At that time I would find myself drifting all the time, as I had no idea as to what happened to

Ray Brown and myself in happeir times

me, to end up in the hospital. I knew the drugs were getting stronger as I felt tired most days. I spent a lot of time laying around on my bed confused and wondering what was going to happen to my army career. The drugs I was taking seemed to make me feel exhausted, but I believe they took the edge off the suicidal thoughts that were also constantly crossing my mind. I didn't know the name of the drugs I was being fed, I only knew I took five a day. I managed a joke one night with the nurse who dispensed the drugs. I asked him if I kept taking my five a day would I be able to leave the hospital. I did not know how long I had been in hospital by then, I guessed at least around six weeks. I must have started to conform to the rules a little better as I was told that I would soon be seen, by an army psychiatrist; a Colonel no less. I behaved the best I could as a drugged up soldier and sure enough a few days later, I got called to the office to meet the Colonel.

That first meeting with him, I told him that I was alright and that I just wanted to go back to a normal unit. He told me that I had had some kind of breakdown and that there was a chance that I may do something to myself or someone else as, not only could I have killed myself, I may have killed someone else. I told him, I was not the type of person to kill someone and I had not thought about killing myself. Of course I was lying about the bit that I had not thought of suicide. I was smart enough not to tell him, I had thought of taking my own life. That would have certainly played into his hands. I wasn't going to give him a reason to discharge me from the army. He asked me if I could remember what had happened to me prior to arriving in the hospital. I told him I didn't have a clue, which at the time was the truth. He then started telling me what he believed had happened. I had apparently, tried to get a weapon and ammunition from the armoury, but had been restrained in the guard room. I told him, I had no recollection of that happening and if I wanted a weapon and ammunition, I would just need to wait until I took the recruits on the firing range. The Colonel then changed tack, and asked if I could remember having a conversation with an officer, prior to going to the armoury. I once again told him the truth as I saw it at the time, I had no memory of any incidents and that I was a very good soldier. He then went on to say, whilst he believed I was a very good soldier, he could not allow me to return to active duty, or at least until they had found out what was wrong with me. I once again told him, I only want to return to duty as the army had become the only thing in my life where I had found love and security. With that, the Colonel told me that was the end of my initial appointment, he just wanted to meet me and introduce himself. He told me that he would see me again in a week or so. Once again I pleaded to go back to my unit, to which he replied, he had to look into my military history to see if he could see anything significant that would have sent me over the edge. I told him there were many things I kept to myself, especially where death was involved.

With that I left and went back to the ward.

I got back to find John by my bunk. He asked me how I got on with the shrink. I just told him the shrink wanted to find out what sent me over the edge and I told John what I told the shrink and that was I didn't have a clue. John asked me if I had been in the hospital before as I seemed to know a lot about the

FLASHBACKS

place. I confided in John that I had been injured in Northern Ireland and I ended up in the same hospital, a couple of years ago. I told him the truth and that I had plastic surgery on my face, new teeth and a bone in my nose. He said, he wouldn't have guessed I had anything done. I joked that I didn't know he loved me that much and it must have worked if he couldn't tell. I didn't go into the details of the incident as I thought John had his own problems. I told John about me and a young paratrooper called Paul, who was also at that time, on ward fourteen, ward fourteen being the plastic surgery ward. As I had been on the ward for about four weeks, young Paul and I had become good buddies. He had been in hospital months and had only been on the plastics ward the last few weeks as prior to that he had been in intensive care. Paul had been blown up and had lost one leg completely and his other leg had been amputated from the knee downwards, so I called him Stumpy. He was on the plastics ward as the doctors were trying to cover his stump with new skin as he had also been badly burned.

I told John, me and Stumpy had become mates in hospital, in the same way John and I had.

He said, 'thanks Corporal.'

I told him he doesn't have to call me Corporal, only if an officer is about or a senior rank to me. Of course his reply was, 'thanks Corporal.'

I knew young John had not been out of training long. John sat with me for the next couple of hours as I swung the lamp, which is the army term for telling stories. The first one I told him was about me and young Paul, when I was in the hospital, the last time.

FLASHBACKS

I went on to say how young Paul had been caught up in a roadside bomb and blown up. I knew his story as there were many soldiers like Paul in the seventies. The fact that he had survived when his mates died, was more to the point, I guess Paul will end up on the crazy ward eventually, perhaps sooner than later. The real shame about it all was that young Paul was only eighteen, having half a leg that was a very messy lump and the other leg totally gone had put him in a wheel chair for the rest of his life. He had been in hospital about four months when I met him, being a paratrooper he was a brave young man.

I thought him a great kid, I said, 'Kid, I was about twenty five myself and had been in the army nearly ten years.' Poor Paul had such courage when he talked to his parents, as they were there quite often, as you would be if that happened to your son – if, of course, the parents gave a toss about you. Personally I hadn't told my mother or family about my injury at that time; I had thought I would wait to go on leave.

At that time after every visit from his parents, I would become his counsellor, trying to cheer him up. Paul would chat away to his parents, he would tell them he was okay, that he was going to be fine and that he was the same person with legs as he was without legs. I don't think they believed him, as I was with him most of the time they came. They sort of visited us both, as we had come from the same camp. I was Paul's buddy and I think they thought I was in a bad way, as my face was covered in bandages and plasters. I looked like a racing car driver with the hood they wore under the helmet.

Paul's mother would always ask to look at Paul's stump, which was like my face, work in progress. His stump looked

FLASHBACKS

like a model of a leg that some kid had made at school. If you can imagine a large joint of meat and you shape it into a leg, that's what Paul was left with. They were trying to take skin from all over his body to cover the stump as it did look a mess. His mother would look and turn away and you could see she was crying. Young Paul saved his tears until they left, he didn't cry in front of them, only after they had gone. I knew he was crying about his leg and his mate that died, as it's what you did as squaddies you couldn't let anyone see what was happening to you, as that would be a sign of weakness.

'It's how we all thought then mate,' I told John, we just got on with it.

I then told John how after visiting time, Paul and I had our own agenda. Official visiting time normally finished around twelve on Sunday, which was when me and Paul started our programme. Although it was a military hospital, in general, servicemen could visit at anytime. We always planned to get rid of visitors by lunch time. At lunch time I would go up to the ward sister, who would normally be Royal Army Medical Corp. I would tell her Paul was a little upset after his parents visit and would it be alright if I pushed him around the hospital grounds for some fresh air. She would always say, 'stick close to the grounds.'

Of we would go, me as the invisible man with my bandages covering my face, I also had a pot on my left wrist, to help with the image. Paul sat on his bum in the wheelchair, with the stump of what used to be his leg sticking out like a battering ram.

It would take us about an hour to reach the pub, situated just off the main road into Woolwich. I told John I couldn't remember the exact location of the pub, but was sure I could find it again if we get a chance to get out. John said, it was against orders and we may get into trouble, I told him, we are soldiers and it was our duty to get into trouble.

I said, you don't have to obey orders all the time John, you have to use your initiative in these matters.' I told him how Paul and I only bought one round in that pub. The locals certainly treated us like heroes, we certainly looked the part.

John asked, 'Did you get into trouble, when you got back to the hospital?'

'Of course not mate,' I told him, 'being good soldiers we always came back after our afternoon session, back on the ward for about six, as the shift changed at six and that was the official time for the afternoon visitors to leave. Paul being only eighteen was generally falling asleep by then pissed and I had my face covered in bandages so they couldn't see how pissed I was. I would help Paul into bed, while the shift was changing then stagger back to my bed.

John was always impressed by anything I said to him; he reminded me of when I was a boy soldier and how I used to be impressed by Sergeant Tom B. I suppose in some ways it was the same, soldiers are only impressed by soldiers.

John asked me, 'If there were any other times that I had been treated in any other military hospitals, in my career.

I told him, a sort of military hospital, more of a sick bay and showed him the scar between my left finger and thumb.

I showed him the fang marks on my left hand where I was bit by a snake. I was in the jungles of Central America. He seemed quite amazed at that, I told him how my job at the time was as a forward air controller. The squadron I was with at that time were a specialist unit of signallers and we were attached to the RAF in Oxfordshire. Although we were based in Oxfordshire, we hardly ever saw England as it seemed we were always away in some part of the world. As was the case when I got bit by the snake, I was in Belize, formally known as British Honduras. The SAS were doing patrols and reconnaissance on the enemy positions. My job was to go into the jungle and provide the communications for various units. I would communicate with the pilots flying the Harriers from airport camp, the Sea Harriers from our aircraft carrier (Ark Royal) and any soldiers in the jungle. To do the job I spent most of my time in Belize in the middle of the jungle. I would liaise with various patrols and basically call up an air strike. It was quite a buzz when you called for an air strike and a few minutes later you have a harrier hovering above you in the middle of nowhere. I could tell John was impressed, himself having only been in the army a few months he had very little experience of such things.

I told him that in the middle of the jungle you need to wrap up well at night with your mosquito net and make sure you check your kit all the time. He would find this out if he did a jungle survival course. I told him about airport camp, the airfield base just outside Belize City, which was the main headquarters and home to all the servicemen stationed in Belize. We did not have a hospital on the main camp, more of a sick bay. If it was a serious injury, I believe they had an operating theatre on the Ark Royal and in the worst case scenario they would fly you to Florida for treatment. In the

FLASHBACKS

army camp they had a sick bay and that's where I ended up after six weeks in the jungle. I told John about being in the Jungle and how every morning we would always check our equipment before getting dressed, mainly because of the scorpions. They would crawl into your kit, especially boots, so you had to check them, turn them upside down and shake anything out of them that shouldn't be there. I wasn't working one day and I decided to chill out as you do in the middle of the jungle, I found myself a nice spot to sunbathe and fell asleep. As I was laying on my army camp bed, about six inches off the ground, I can only assume that the snake that bit me thought my hand resting on the ground was a meal as I woke up to feel the pain in my left hand and fortunately able to see what had just bit me.

It was sheer luck that I had my machete by my right hand and managed to chop the snake in half, giving me the name of the snake that had just bit me. I became a CASEVAC as they call it in the army, Casualty evacuation. I was becoming ill but was able to communicate my situation and was fully conscious up to getting on the helicopter they had sent to fly me out of the jungle. Having the snake made life easier to get the antidote for the poison. I was told by a mate that I was flown to the Ark Royal to get the initial treatment for the bite, before being flown back to airport camp and placed in the sick bay. I do not remember much after getting on the chopper to leave the jungle, I remember receiving an injection to combat the snake bite but I still ended up a sick and crazy person for a while.

I told John about the sick bay I had ended up in, I said it wasn't a hospital like the one we were both in at that time.

FLASHBACKS

It was an old steel hut, like something from the fifties, with a red cross on the door. It was a corrugated steel building, like the army used to have years ago. The building itself had two layers of corrugated steel, I think they built them like that in Belize, as the heat could be absorbed by the outer layer.

I couldn't resist telling John about the day in that tin sick bay. After a few days I had started to feel a little better and although I was the only soldier in the sick bay, I did manage to find some friends. I kept having visitors, I couldn't see them, but I knew they were there as I could hear them running up and down, in between the layers of steel. I knew instinctively what they were as there were hundreds around camp. They were chit chats as we called them, little lizards that scurried about all over the place. We would try to catch them, by grabbing their tails, if you managed to grab hold of their tail or put your boot on the tail they would just run off, leaving their tails behind them. Well you have to entertain yourselves as squaddies with no booze and nothing to do except play soldiers.

Being in the sick bay I was getting quite bored, so to entertain myself as I wasn't allowed out of bed I had found a hole about an inch diameter in the inner layer of the tin hut, just behind my bed. I pushed a very small piece of chicken through the hole and waited to hear the scurrying. Sure enough after a few minutes, I heard the scurry then the meat was whisked off. I don't know if it was the snake bite that was still making me delirious or just daft, but that little lizard became my mate, as all my mates were out in the jungle playing soldiers with the SAS and the resident infantry battalion.

FLASHBACKS

The day after, the medic walked in and told me the medical officer would be over to see me after lunch and I may be able to get back to work.

Lunch came and as per normal, I decided to save some for Charlie as I had given my mate a name. I just assumed Charlie the lizard was a male, although I had never saw him. I would lie on my side with my back to the door and saying, 'come on Charlie, come on Charlie,' with my arm stretched out to push the piece of meat through the hole for Charlie. To anyone looking on, it looked like I was talking to no-one, just blurting 'out come on Charlie'.

I heard the door go and the medic walked up to me and told me the medical officer had just seen me talking to myself and had since told him to tell me, to stay in bed for another couple of days.' He thought I had gone round the twist.

SAS dropped off in Belizean Jungle, I am airlifted out after snake bite.

FLASHBACKS

Young John laughed at my story about Belize and with that I told him I was tired and I was going to get my head down. I said I hope you have not been too bored listening to my war stories mate.

No Corporal,' he said, 'it's really interesting, can we chat later?'

I said, 'Of course John, and for God's sake, call me Mick.'

I was starting to get attached to John. I felt sorry for him, he wasn't like most soldiers, he was quiet and sensitive and I don't know how the hell he ended up in the army, especially the infantry. He seemed as though he may have been better suited to being a clerk in the Intelligence Corps, as he was quite bright.

After John left me to rest, I once again started to daydream as I never read books and wasn't that bothered about the TV unless it was top of the pops or anything with tits in it, I didn't bother watching. I felt a little down and was thinking about myself stuck in the hospital. The only thing to do was to lie on my bed and wait for an orderly to come around with the drugs trolley. So I had all the time in the world to think. Having just thought about how John ended up in the infantry, I remembered when I went to the careers office in Sheffield. I nearly ended up in the Navy as that's the first guy I saw. He looked at me and said army downstairs, navy and air force upstairs.

The Army guy got hold of me, he wasn't very bright I thought, as he said, 'Over here son.' I recognised his cap badge and knew he was in the infantry. Much to my embarrassment he was in a Yorkshire regiment and he was seriously thick, or so I thought. He told me to sit down and take a test to find out what regiment I would be allowed to join, I told him I would like to join the Paras.

He said, 'You can do that anytime you like, when you are in the army, you can go to the airborne.' I sat down and took the test. He told me I was a very intelligent young man,' as I got one hundred percent on the test. Being intelligent was news to me as I had left school without taking any exams. I knew I was sharp as I could work out how much money my mother had won when she gambled, which was quite often. But I didn't know I was intelligent, I thought that was a name for posh kids who went to grammar school. Anyway he said I could go in any regiment I wanted too.

'The paras would be okay but he made me aware of the fact that I was only just five feet tall and weighed about eight stone, He said, I am not sure you would make it for a couple of years and then if you fail, you could end up in the infantry.

I said, 'What about the Royal Corps of Transport? I wouldn't mind being a driver.'

He said again, 'That would not tax you, have you ever thought about the Royal Signals?' He said, 'You could become a radio telegraphist'; TG operator as it was known.

I opted for the Signals as he told me I could always go to the Paras at a later date. He said if he had had the option he would have joined something like the Signals, as he was in the signals platoon in his battalion and he loved it. What swung it for me was that if I joined the Signals, I would get attached to lots of different regiments. He said the signals were one of the most important jobs in the army, as without communications, the army cannot work. He also said that I would get a City and

FLASHBACKS

Guilds qualification in Telecommunications, which would be a recognised qualification when I left the army. He said he'd been an infantry man for twenty years, and all he could do when he left the army was get a course in plumbing, bricklaying or some other physical job, or go into security.

That swung it for me and that's how I ended up at that army apprentice college. It turned out the guy in the careers office was right. Prior to the situation I was now in, stuck in hospital, I had been all over the world, with so many different regiments.

I once again fell to sleep that night, trying to remember what had happened to me, to end up in hospital, I just could not remember a thing.

I don't know if it was because I had been having a laugh with John talking about Belize or it could have been the effect from the drugs, whatever it was, I had fallen asleep and in my subconscious, I felt down and suicidal. I was not sure if I was dreaming or awake, either way I had this strange feeling of guilt coming over me. I had done nothing wrong to feel guilty, so why would I feel so guilty. I just could not understand what was happening to me, it was as though I was wide awake. I remembered falling asleep, thinking that it must be the drugs and I would be fine when I got out of the hospital.

Again I didn't know if it was the drugs or my mind playing games with me, but the thoughts of guilt came in my dreams. I effectively started to dream about my life, I guess as I had fallen asleep thinking about when I joined up. My dreams were real and factual that night.

FLASHBACKS

I remembered being at the army apprentice college as a boy soldier. After I had got through my initial three months, I ended up in a squadron, with my best mate Ray Brown. I ended up getting roped into athletics, I never thought I would be up to much, as I was such a midget when I joined up. Even after six months as a boy soldier, I was sixteen and I was still only about five foot two inches tall. I had put on a little weight as by then I was around nine stone, which I guess was an improvement. The one thing I could do was run quite fast, something I had learned by being chased by the police on numerous occasions. Luckily they never caught me as I found out from the army careers that you cannot join the army if you have a police record. That aside, I could run and I was also very good at sit ups and dips and that sort of exercise; consequently I had strong stomach muscles. The running fast and the strong muscles were all I needed for the event I was asked to have a go at in athletics. It turned out that all that running from the police and jumping up over walls and garden fences had trained me for the pole vault.

I was entered, to do the pole vault for the squadron athletics. I had an eleven foot aluminium pole, it was only about an inch in diameter, not at all like the fibreglass poles they had in the Olympics. It turned out I didn't need the fibre glass pole as I had a go and found it quite easy.

The day came for the inter squadron athletics and of course I won, clearing ten feet four inches. That was enough to win me the inter squadron pole vault, the winner of which got to represent the college in the army junior championships that took place every year at Aldershot.

FLASHBACKS

I must have been laughing in my sleep as I remembered winning the pole vault at Harrogate and getting to go down to the army championships. The athletics team were booked on a train to Aldershot and we would be away for a week. The funny thing was every contestant had to take their own piece of equipment, which was okay for the discus, shot, etc. I had to manoeuvre a long pole around the stations. It was real fun on the underground trying to get through to Waterloo, where we would catch the Aldershot train. I nearly speared loads of people, which everyone seemed to enjoy.

I went on to win the army junior championship, clearing the dizzy height of eleven feet three inches, which was no mean feat with an eleven foot pole.

Life changed for me after that in the squadron as not only had I got lots of mates but, I had impressed my troop Sergeant Tom B. I was also doing well with my trade training. I had mastered the Morse code and could do about fifteen words a minute. My job also meant I had to learn to type. The two skills were supposed to take me two years to master, as that was how long I would be at the army apprentice college. I mastered them in my first year and as such I would have had nothing to do for two hours every day in my second year at the college. So I was asked to move up a grade from Radio Operator to Telegraphist, which meant I would have to do Morse faster and basically everything else faster. I was pleased as it also meant I would get paid more as it was a vast upgrade from a B to an A trade.

The fact that I only got three pounds thirteen shillings at the time as wages didn't come into it. I was never worried about money and sent most of my wages home to my mother via a post office book. She could draw two pounds two shillings every week. I used to give her all my wages before I joined the army, so I never got used to having money.

As I was the chief feeder of the family before I joined the army, I wanted to make sure my mother had money to feed my younger brother and sister, at least once a week. Providing food for my family was another job I took on before I enlisted. From being about twelve years old, I would do the shopping for my mother. She would give me two shilling or around ten pence as it is now, I would go to the supermarket, walk around helping myself and basically steal about three pounds worth of food. Not only did I feed the family I would also get to keep the two shillings. I got a paper round in the mornings, so on my way back to the paper shop I would fetch three pints of milk back for my mother, all stolen on my round. I never took milk from the same house twice and I only took one if they had more than one delivered. Even at twelve years old I had a conscience, I couldn't see a family not having their breakfast. I believed it was only fair to take the milk as my round included most of the posh houses in Rotherham.

That night passed, having fallen asleep thinking about my joining the Army. It was the army that woke me. It was the army physical training corps, they had decided that maybe all the poor guys in hospital may be missing physical training. Maybe that was the reason we were all messed up.

As it happened I had missed the physical side of army life, as before I ended up in hospital, I did remember I was an instructor with Leadership troop. The troop consisted of a sergeant major, ex SAS, an officer who was a fanatical captain, who loved nothing more than physical training; so much so that he went and did the marine commando course at Lypstone. There were two corporals; me and another guy called Mick W. He had been in the army a lot longer than me so between us we used to do the physical training, command tasks, which is basically how to get across a river with a plank of wood and a rope sort of thing, and the admin side of the troop, arranging exercises and visits. Mick W did the more mundane shit and I did all the physical.

This course was designed for men wishing to be an officer in the army, but either they came from a poor background, which made them very intelligent but no money in the family, or they came from a very rich family and had lots of money, but the candidate was either spoiled or thick. A lot of the latter types had connections and I believe it was the connections that would get them on the course. The poor candidates were always better, but the chances of passing were less as they had no connections.

There would only ever be around twenty people on a course and perhaps only two would pass. We never really found out who passed as we were just pawns in the game, which is something I found out later. I was starting to wonder if that had been part of my breakdown, as that was the last job I remember having.

It was quite good, as a unit, we were quite independent and no one bothered us.

Those potential officers would arrive at Darlington Station and I would be there to meet them off the trains. One particular day my boss Captain H, said, 'Corporal Will,' which I believe he called me because he couldn't call me Mick. He said, 'we have a Lord on the next course Corporal and we don't want any of the other candidates to feel inferior so if you could keep it to yourself.'

I arrived at the station and as normal the candidates were mainly waiting at the clock in the station. I was there with my mill board checking off names. Brown, yes corporal, Smith, yes corporal, and so on, you always knew the poor people as they called you corporal. The rich guys never acknowledged your rank as they had it in their heads that they were going to be officers. That day was no exception, only it was the Lord who got up my back straight away. He had turned up to join the army in full Scottish regalia, i.e. kilt, sporran, glengarry. I thought, what the fuck have we got here. I shouted his name and he of course went, 'Here.' I of course went, 'Here what?'

I heard a mumbled, Corporal.' I had to call them Mister, this guy was Mister B. I believe his father was an Earl and a direct descendant of some famous Scotsman.

I remembered what the boss had told me about not letting the others know he was a Lord. I just asked them all to follow me towards the waiting minibus. As I was walking backwards, I turned to Mr B and said, that includes you too Mr B, at the same time bowing every few seconds and saying, 'hurry along your highness, we don't want to miss the bus.'

Everyone else burst into laughter and Mr B clammed up like the spoiled brat he was.

I am not sure whether it was, whilst I was running that potential officer course that I cracked up, as I still had no idea why I was in hospital. I did remember his course as part of my

FLASHBACKS

job was to give them some shit, in the way of training of course.

To be an instructor I had done an abseiling and mountaineering instructor's course in Scotland, as well as a canoe instructor's course. Part of the potential officer course involved taking the troop to the Lake District for mountaineering, canoeing and basic yomping. It was my job to do those skills, as it had been my job to get them fit before we went to the lakes, which I did by taking them on yomps and runs with full kit. That was how I found out if any of them had any balls and which of them were the quitters. I always reported my findings to the boss, but I felt it was out of his hands, whether someone passed or failed. He had some say but I believe the decision as to who passed or failed had already been discussed by the powerful friends of the candidates. Like if your father is a lord, you have got more chance than if your father is a miner. I knew that for a fact as by a strange coincidence, whilst showing the potential officers photographs of the first potential officer course at that camp. I noticed my older brother in the photos, he had been on the course many years prior to my being there. I believe he only failed, because he was from a working class background.

I remembered a particular day in a place called Cathedral Caves, not far from Coniston Water where we were camping. I had set up an abseil above the caves so it was around one hundred feet down into the cave. The idea being I would be on the top with the potential officers, I set up a belay and would send them down one at a time. I was just sending a massive guy down, he was saying, 'I'm awfully sorry Corporal but I don't think I can do this.'

FLASHBACKS

He was at the time being held by the chap on the belay, who was secured to a massive tree, as such he couldn't really fall that far. At that moment, I thought about the possibility of one day, the potential officer I had hanging over the edge of the cave would be my leader. With that in mind, I listened to his begging for me to pull him back up, as he was afraid. I thought of sergeant B and the punch in the stomach. I then wondered what the sergeant might have done to a normal recruit. I then kicked the potential officers feet off the edge and watch him fall about five feet. He was in no danger but he still screamed like a little girl. I leaned over the edge and told him that his only way down was now on the abseil. I didn't care how long he was going to take as far as I was concerned we were leaving in two hours and he could stay there. He then accepted his fate and slowly abseiled down into the cave. It took him over ten minutes to get down, something I would have done in ten seconds, so I guessed he was never going to be a leader. He came back up and the cheeky bastard said to me, 'That was super Corporal.'

I said, 'I am pleased you enjoyed it,' and sent him down again, just to make sure he wasn't lying. I did enjoy going to the Lakes as Mick the other corporal and I had it all planned, especially the twelve mile trek over Scafell Pike. Scafell was the highest mountain and as such it was a bit of a test. Mick and I had been over it many times and although it was our job to follow behind the potential officers, we rarely did. We would set them off in groups of four, with ten minutes between each group and after we had watched the last group go out of sight, we would then set off. Normally one of us would follow the

FLASHBACKS

last group, just keeping out of sight, whilst the other instructor drove to the other end of the mountain and trekked up a mile or so to see the groups coming in. That day being a sunny day, Mick and I decided we would leave them to their own devices. We both jumped into our Land Rover and set off to the other end of the mountain, to a little pub we knew in the valley. We were not totally irresponsible as we had made sure the man in the leading group could map read. The groups always met up on the march as each group tried to catch up to the next. It would take the groups around four hours to reach their objective. It would take us thirty minutes to drive to the same objective, the little pub in the valley. Mick and I had four or five beers, sat in the beer garden as we awaited sight of the groups. It was not that reckless as the pub was next to the camp site we would be camping in that night. That part of the exercise was always a long couple of days for me and Mick. I remember that first day after the groups had completed Scafell, we would let them relax with a couple of beers. Then the next day we would send them back over Scafell as we recovered from our marathon session.

With such memories entering my mind all the time, I once again returned to the present, for me that morning in the hospital. It turned out, the physical exercise we were going to do, was not so demanding, we were going to walk around the grounds. We couldn't do much else as most of the guys on the ward, had no kit. Nearly all of us had been escorted to the hospital in the clothes we were wearing and the only other kit we had was the pyjamas they issued us on arrival. The hospital staff must have assumed I was going to be in hospital a while

FLASHBACKS

as my army issue suitcase, full of civilian clothes, running gear and a set of uniforms arrived at the side of my bed, within a couple of days of my arriving in hospital.

That afternoon I was told I had another appointment with Colonel D, my newly designated shrink. He asked me about my childhood and I told him that my childhood had nothing to do with whatever had happened to me, as I had been in the army twelve years. I told him I just wanted to go back to my unit and be a soldier again as I was getting more and more angry being in that hospital. He once again asked me if I had thought of taking my own life.

I said, 'Doesn't everyone think that?' as the truth was that I had began to think about suicide a lot. I told him, up to joining the army I had never thought about suicide, it had only come on since I joined the army.

He said that my army record told him that when I left boy service, I was posted to Germany. He asked me what happened when I got to Germany.

I said it was me and my best mate Ray Brown, we were posted to the 7th Armoured Brigade in northern Germany. He asked me to start at the beginning and tell him what happened to me in my first few months in that brigade.

I went on to explain how Ray and I arrived in Germany as two young seventeen years old boys, very nervous about what was expected of us, as we were by then proper soldiers, or so we thought.'

The first thing we had to do was report to the Regimental Sergeant Major, God to everyone in the squadron. We were both now a part of that squadron and as such we were stood outside the RSM's office, waiting to be introduced. He had a massive red rat about two feet high painted on his door with his name underneath it, Regimental Sergeant Major Bres.

We marched inside and he didn't look up for a few moments, he then stood up and with great pride in his voice turned to me and said, 'Do you know what that is on my door?' pointing at the red painted rat.

Being me, I couldn't resist it, I said, 'Is it a squirrel sir?'

He picked up the phone and phoned Sgt Len who was the guard commander, 'Sgt Len get your ass up here.'

The sergeant arrived and the RSM turned to Ray and said, 'Do you know what that is on my door?'

Ray said, 'It's a rat sir.'

'You stay here,' the RSM told Ray. 'Sgt Len take this young man and put him in jail and give him something to read that may enlighten him into what squadron he is now serving with, before I put him in front of the Commanding Officer.'

I was locked up and given some books about the squadron, so my first few days were spent in jail in Germany. I was sat in jail thinking, If only my mother could see me now, she was frightened of me being sent to Germany. It was funny when I told her I was being posted to Germany. I said, 'Mum I have been sent to Germany.'

I remembered my mother's reply came from a Greek woman who had lost family and fought the Germans. She just said, 'Kill 'em Mickey, kill the bastards.'

I said, 'I don't think we are allowed to do that now mother, the war has been ended nearly thirty years.'

I started to read the book about the unit I had come to.

FLASHBACKS

It was formed from the 79th Armoured Division, which was the unit commanded by Lord Montgomery of Alamein. I didn't know at the time but I would cross the history of Monte as he was known later on in my career when Monte dies.

I found out that the red rats were known as jerboa rats and they were the emblem of the armoured Division. Every soldier that served in the brigade would have the red rats insignia fitted to their uniforms. Having read some of the history of the desert rats, I could see why the RSM was a little annoyed.

Just in case I didn't read the book about the 79th Armoured Division to learn about the Desert Rats, the RSM had told the guard commander that at the weekends, I would have to report to the guard house, where I would be given Brasso to clean all the brass rats that were all over the place. Then I would be given the red paint to paint all the red rats that were also situated in every part of the camp.

'That was my first two weeks in the regular Army,' I told the Colonel who was now my shrink.

'Carry on,' he told me, so I then went into my next few weeks, not that there was a lot to tell as my first couple of months in the big Army were done on guard or jankers.

I started to think that the RSM had it in for me, as he didn't like my spirit. My being a little stupid didn't help. In the army as soon as you come out of a building you should have your beret on. I had just finished my jankers and was thinking I will be able to join one of the troops soon and get my armoured vehicle licence, track licence as it was known.

That particular day, I had just come out of the accommodation block, I had my beret in my hand and the RSM was just coming out of the HQ building across the square from me. He raised his hand in the air, which looked to me like he was waving at me, so I just put my hand in the air to say hi. I thought he has obviously forgiven me for the rat and I was just thinking he doesn't seem a bad bloke. I was just on my way to the guardroom to see Sergeant Len as that day was to be my last on guard duty and jankers. I got there and Sergeant Len, said, 'I don't know what you have done now son, but the RSM has just phoned down and told me he has just given you five more days on jankers.'

I told the sergeant that I had just seen the RSM across the square and I thought he was waving to me, as he put his hand up with the palm facing me. He laughed out loud and said, 'You fucking idiot, that's how the RSM dishes out jankers. You have now got five more days, for not having your beret on when you left the accommodation block.'

Sergeant Len didn't give me too much shit in those five days, as I think he felt sorry for me, so I did my jankers and managed to get posted to Alpha Troop, with my best mate Ray.

At last I thought I am going to be playing soldiers at least it had to be better than guard duty and jankers.

Ray and I stuck together as a lot of the guys in the troop thought that because we were straight out of boy service they had the right to mess us about. Not much difference to before I joined the army and worked in the steelworks. I went and got the left handed screw driver and the chequered paint. Most of the soldiers had been in the army years and loved it in Germany, as it was heaven for guys who wanted to get pissed and play soldiers without any worries. I kept thinking I wanted to go

FLASHBACKS

and do some proper soldiering as the thought of just playing soldiers didn't seem that brilliant.

Little did I know as I later found out that there are as many soldiers dying on exercise or in accidents, as there are that die in action. I would also find out later that there are as many, if not more, soldiers committing suicide than dying in action. At that time the only action we had as soldiers were fighting the IRA in Northern Ireland. Even as a boy soldier we knew only too well the risks of going to Northern Ireland. As the troubles had just kicked off again in 1969 which was the year I signed up in the army. My boy troop, junior sergeant had gone to Ireland on his first posting and got killed. As he was the first boy soldier from the college, they made a big thing of it and named a cup after him.

The Colonel I was talking to said, 'So, you experienced losing someone you knew as a boy soldier?'

I said, 'Yes sir, but I wasn't that upset as I knew him, but we were not real close buddies and I didn't witness him killed. At that time I just thought it was part of the job. I had never felt I wanted to kill any one as a child. I knew I was not bothered about dying, but after he was murdered I did believe I could have quite easily killed the people who killed him. Also at the time I remember thinking that if I died trying to right the injustice of his murder, I could live with that as the thing that always crosses your mind as a soldier, even as a boy soldier is the thought you may have to kill someone some day. After his murder I could understand my mother's story of all the family she had lost fighting Germans. I felt a lot more for my mother and her losses than I did with the death of the boy sergeant in

FLASHBACKS

Northern Ireland. If anything, I felt the most saddened for his parents and family. I actually thought dying might be a relief to some people, especially my mother, having watched her live her life in constant torment. She would constantly tell me that she wanted to be with her dead mother. Even as a young boy I remember promising to take her there. I promised her I would find where her mother was buried and put her to rest in the same grave. I guess it was a lot to put on my shoulders, but I loved her dearly and it always seemed to pep her up. At that time, I couldn't imagine what my mother had been through during the war, I just knew she suffered mentally every day. I told the Colonel one of the stories our mother told us, the day she saw her brother executed by the Germans. She was only seventeen years old and lived with her family in a small village called Dara. At that time her father was a farmer, he owned a great deal of land and her brother was a policeman, like a village copper. His boss was a man called George who was the inspector, later to marry my mother's sister. My mother hated George and when I met him, later in my army career I saw why. When my mother's brother was killed by the Germans, he had been captured, along with most of the men from the village. My mother didn't tell us what happened. I found out later from a relative in Greece as I visited our family grave in the village. There is a statue there to this day with the names of the people from the village that were either killed in action fighting the Germans or executed, after being captured. It was widely believed that the resistance group my mother and her brother were fighting with had been betrayed. It was also known that my mother's brother, whose name was also George

FLASHBACKS

did not want his sister Helen to marry George. He knew his boss was not good enough to marry his sister as he knew him to be a bad man, constantly using his power as the police inspector to go with other women. There was a great deal of bad blood between the two men, as my uncle watched the inspector feather his own nest. He also didn't like the fact that he was too friendly with the Germans as the Greeks in the villages believed there was an informer amongst them. They suspected the inspector, but without proof the resistance could not kill him, they would have done as they killed many collaborators.

The day my mother's brother was captured, they were ambushed and had to surrender. The Germans took the fighters to their barracks to await interrogation by the Gestapo. My mother was a gorgeous young woman and with her looks had enticed many German soldiers into an ambush. By the time she was seventeen years old, she had already fought in the

7th Armoured Brigade, camouflaged.

resistance. She had already witnessed many of her family and friends being killed, either fighting the Germans or executed by them. Many of the Greeks were just executed as a reprisal for any resistance activity against the Germans. Hence my mother hated the Germans with a passion.

When she had heard about her brother being captured, she went to the German barracks. My mother would do anything for her brother George as he was her hero and she wanted to discuss how she could help him escape.

The German soldiers spoke to my mother, telling her, they would let her see her brother, but on the condition, she agreed to have sex with the two guards. My mother did what they asked as she was already hardened from the war and didn't really care about herself. Sadly the Germans had their way with her, they sent for her brother George who was by that time black and blue from the interrogation. They told my mother, "we told you we would let you see your brother and we Germans keep our word".

They dragged her badly beaten brother past her, she shouted, 'Sagapo, I love you George my darling brother.' He managed to say the same back to her in Greek. They dragged him straight past my mother and tied him to a post and executed him. My mother had told me that story after I had been home on leave from Germany. Had she told me the story before I went to Germany I would not have found it so amusing, as it now made sense, why she hated the Germans so much.

The Colonel said, 'Your childhood must have upset you, all these things that happened to your mother.' I told him I was proud of my mother and our family, we may have had it rough,

FLASHBACKS

but we were loved. I told him I had nothing from my childhood that bothered me.

He went on to ask me about any other deaths of soldiers that I had experienced as a soldier in the army. I jokingly replied, something along the lines of, where do you want me to start sir?

I did start, I said, 'That's easy Sir.' I told him I had been on guard duty and jankers for most of my first few weeks in the army. I managed to escape those guard duties and jankers by going on exercise (or manoeuvres as they are better known). Our job in Germany was to provide the communications for the brigade as it went on exercise. Our radios were mounted in the backs of armoured personnel carriers. We would be on exercise for maybe six weeks at a time, driving and moving location all the time. Most of our exercises took place on Luneburg Heath which was the main training area in that part of Germany. There was a large barracks in a place called Hohne, it was where most of the 7th armoured brigade was stationed. Ironically it used to be the headquarters of Adolf Hitler and now it was the home of the British army. The nearest village to Hohne was Bergen, which itself was next to Belsen, the famous concentration camp. I told the Colonel that was my first experience of death as a soldier, visiting the camp at Belsen. I was only seventeen and I could not believe what I could see on display, the photos of the mass graves with skeletons.

The Colonel said, he knew about Belsen and that he was more interested in my personal experiences. I told the Colonel that although that was my first experience of seeing mass death in detail, it did link in to my first deaths of British soldiers on manoeuvres. As the manoeuvres took place on a training area, a few miles from Belsen. I went on to talk about the three soldiers that got killed on that exercise. I explained to him how on exercise in Germany, we got moved around, from dusk to dawn and how we all became exhausted. In general at night we would put up small tents to sleep in but if you were knackered you didn't bother with the tents, you could just use your poncho as a ground sheet. We would just put some ferns down, put the ground sheet on top and roll-out sleeping bag. Most of the time, we were so tired we could fall asleep stood up.

7th Armoured Brigade headquarters

FLASHBACKS

To that end, having 432s or armoured personnel carriers as they are better known, a lot of the guys including myself would get our sleeping bags out and as it was quite warm under the 432s, we would get in our sleeping bags and roll under the vehicles to go to sleep. If you crawled under the front of the vehicle you had the heat from the engine and there was about a foot between the under belly of the vehicle and the ground, as the tracks were quite big.

Although it was frowned upon as being lazy, no one had thought it was dangerous. Until of course the three soldiers died, screaming in agony. We learned of it because we had to send the message on to headquarters. They had pulled in to a wooded location and set up camp. This entailed setting up camouflage netting and communication equipment. Most of us would try and park our armoured vehicles between the trees. That enabled you to use fewer poles for camouflage and made it easier to set up camp. Those three guys had been having problems with the engine of their armoured vehicle. Their vehicle was broken down in a wooded area and the engine was being worked on by a set of engineers from the Royal Electrical Mechanical Engineers, also known as the REME. They had the engine stripped down and were working on it, so basically it couldn't drive. Even if it could have been driven, the outcome would have been the same for the three guys who had gone to sleep under the 432. They were all knackered as they were not going anywhere quickly so they got their heads down to sleep. Unfortunately for them, it never stopped raining for a few hours and as the rest of their squadron had moved location it was only the REME or mechanics that were left to fix their vehicle. It was those guys who raised the alarm and tried in vain to extract the three young soldiers from under the vehicle as it sunk further and further in to the ground, crushing the life out of those soldiers. They tried to dig the men out as the fifty ton vehicle slowly crushed the life out of the three soldiers. I told the Colonel I think I would have rather gone in the Gas chamber than get crushed to death slowly with tons of armour on top of me.

With that he said, 'We will leave it for now Corporal.' I again told the Colonel that I was fine and once again asked if I could go back to my unit. I said I didn't feel like killing myself, I just wanted to go back to work. I knew I was lying as I had started to feel quite suicidal, even though I was only talking about things that I didn't believe had had any effect on me.

432 Personel Carrier, similar to the one the three soldiers slept under.

FLASHBACKS

I thought if I told the Colonel what was really on my mind when he asked me about my first death as a soldier, I would be getting near to having a reason for being in hospital. I also thought if I opened up as to what was going through my mind; the thoughts of injustice and suicide, I would never get back to my unit.

I went back to the ward and decided to try and become the soldier I was before I had ended up in hospital. I decided that I was going to train and get myself fit. Having been in hospital weeks, months, the lack of activity was starting to get me down. I don't know if it was the medication or just idleness, but all these fit soldiers were turning into fat unfit young men. I got permission to go running around the football pitch, as that was part of the hospital grounds.

I told young John that I was going to get myself fit. If he wished, he could come and train with me. He had a stop watch on his watch, so he set it up to time himself and me running around the football pitch.

After two laps, John said, 'I can't go on Corporal.' He sat down by the goal post and just timed me running around the track. Every time I went past him, he would say, 'one minute, or whatever length of time it had taken me to do the lap. The one thing I could still do was run, as I had had plenty of practice running cross country for my unit.

After about twenty laps, roughly five miles, I sat down knackered, my back against the same goal post young John had his back too.

John asked me what the shrink had been talking to me about. I said I thought he was trying to work out what had

FLASHBACKS

happened with me to flip, so I guess he wanted to go through my career to maybe identify what would make a man flip.

'I think the shrink is treading careful with me, maybe it's because I had stopped behaving badly like young Rifleman T. or it could be that because I had already attacked one officer, he may be afraid to push me too far. I can sort of understand that part myself,' I told John, I cannot identify what it is, that is leading me to self-destruct, but I do feel like a ticking time bomb waiting to explode. I guess they must know that, hence all the sedation, like nearly all the guys on the ward.'

He asked me how old I was when I saw my first soldier die. I told him I had sent many messages with regards to soldiers dying, as part of my job when I first went to Germany, especially when I was working part time in the communications centre for the brigade. As such I was sending messages all over the place regarding soldiers dying. I told him of the guys sleeping under the armoured personnel carriers, I told him of the poor guy who drove his tank into a swamp and couldn't get out as he was trapped in the driver's seat. He apparently drowned in the mud. I remembered that one in particular as it happened at three in the morning and I had received a flash message. As a flash message, I had fifteen minutes to despatch the message onwards, so the police would get the message in England and go around to the poor guy's family and inform them of his death. I told him there are as many soldiers dying, without being in action, as there are dying in action. I didn't know how many exactly but from the messages I would be sending there were probably more dying at that time from accidents. At that time the only war we had going on was with

FLASHBACKS

the IRA in Northern Ireland. I always remembered the guy in the tank as I didn't pass the message on for over an hour as I had fallen asleep. My excuse was that I was tired due to being on and off guard duty and being on jankers. It was no excuse really and I probably deserved the fourteen days in jail I got for falling asleep whilst on duty.

I told John 'It never happened again, so it was a good lesson to learn as I was only just eighteen. I went on to tell John about the time just after my eighteenth birthday. It was still the early seventies, I had been in Germany from leaving Boys College and all I was doing there was manoeuvres, guard duty and getting pissed. It came up on daily orders that a volunteer was required to go to Northern Ireland as the radio operator-come-communications guy for the commanding officer of the Royal Green Jackets. I thought I had nothing else to do except playing soldiers in Germany, so much to everyone's surprise I had volunteered. The Green Jackets were one of the infantry battalions who formed part of the seventh armoured brigade. They were based at Celle which was about fifteen miles away. I was a little apprehensive as at that time in Northern Ireland nearly every regiment or battalion who went on a tour of duty lost soldiers. Being a Yorkshire man, I had loads of mates in the Yorkshire infantry battalions. You had regiments like the Green Howards, the Duke of Wellington regiment; a mate of mine had joined the Dukes as they were known from school, another joined another Yorkshire Regiment, the Prince of Wales own Regiment.

The Green Howards were sometimes known as the falling plates, when they did a tour of duty in Northern Ireland, as at that time they used to lose lots of men. Falling plates were L shaped pieces of steel that soldiers would use to shoot at on the firing range, long before they had normal targets to shoot at. The plates would stand up and when you hit them with a bullet they would make a loud ping sound then fall over, hence falling plates became the nickname for battalions who lost lots of men on tour.

I would not have volunteered if the tour was with any of those Yorkshire regiments. The Green Jackets were in my opinion a good regiment. They were mainly Londoners in that 1st Battalion. A lot of men joined up purely because the Royal Green Jackets as they were known had a good reputation and lots of the guys in that battalion were real clued up soldiers. I was quite impressed when I got to the battalion, doing pre Northern Ireland training. They had different specialists attached to the battalion when they went off on tour. Apart from myself there were specialist medics from the Medical Corps.

I then went on to tell John about the first soldier I was close too, as he died. I had been in Northern Ireland about four weeks and I was based in a place called Hasting Street, It used to be an old police station, it was just off the Falls Road in Belfast, not far from the Divis flats and the Shankhill, which at that time was not a healthy place to do a tour. The soldier who died had just been been out with another guy on a dispatch job to Lisburn. It was normal procedure at that time that you would always have an escort or another soldier with you if you went out of the Barracks. To that degree I had a young Infantryman with me as we went in the army issue Ford Escort, to Lisburn.

FLASHBACKS

We had no problems going to Lisburn, it had been my first time out in civilian clothes, with a 9 mm Browning Pistol stuck down the back of my trousers, I felt quite excited to be doing a real job, instead of playing soldiers in Germany. The excitement was to increase quite quickly after we had returned from Lisburn. I had just parked the Escort up in the compound and walked across to the entrance to our barracks. I believe the part of the building we were based in, was in fact the old garages for the police station. The entrance was a roller shutter door, which was kept open most of the time and just at the side of the door was an unloading bay. I had left the young rifleman who had been to Lisburn with me, sat in the car. He was filling out the mileage forms inside the vehicle, something you had to do with every military vehicle. I walked over to the entrance and stood in front of the unloading bay. At the same time there was a young Green Jacket rifleman, who had just got out of another vehicle. He came up and stood at the side of me as we both unloaded our weapons in the sand pit just outside the entrance to our headquarters. To unload the self-loading rifles which were the infantry mans weapon at that time, you basically cock the gun, which means pulling back the firing mechanism, then take off the magazine, holding the bullets. You then look in to the breach and squeeze the trigger, if nothing happens, you put the magazine back on to your weapon, apply the safety catch and your weapon is clear. If for some reason your weapon is not clear, when you squeeze the trigger there would be a bang as any bullet left in your rifle would be fired into the sand pit. I had arrived at the sand pit a fraction of a second before the rifleman, as I had a 9 mm pistol, unloading my weapon was

FLASHBACKS

a lot easier. Although the unloading drill for a pistol is the same as a rifle. With the pistol being small, the drill was much quicker. I had just unloaded my pistol and walked two paces into the building, when I heard the shot. The noise made me jump, lucky I thought no one had seen me jump, so I went to keep walking into the building, thinking that was not very good for a rifleman to have a bullet in his weapon. I was just thinking what a loser when I heard a thud behind me, a sound that stayed with me the rest of my army career. It was the noise of the young rifleman's rifle and magazine hitting the ground followed by the thud of the rifleman. I turned around instinctively and ran the couple of yards to the rifleman, who was by then laying motionless. I grabbed him by his blood soaked collar and dragged him a yard into the building, at the same time trying to see where we were getting shot at from. I shouted, 'Medic!' as I dragged the young man further inside the building, trying to get him nearer to safety. I know he did not die instantly as when I was dragging him into the building, the blood was squirting out of his neck, it was only a matter of seconds before he died as I watched him take a deep breath, more of a gasp for breath and then the blood stopped pumping. By then I had stopped looking from where the shot had come from as I was more interested in trying to help the young soldier, I say young he was probably my age at the time. As I turned him around to try some first aid, I could see where the bullet had entered his head and where it had come out his neck, which was where the blood had been pumping from a few seconds ago. There was a bit of panic, as soldiers appeared by my side and a medic was shoving a dressing into the neck wound and trying to help the soldier, he tried, but you knew it was too late. A couple of soldiers in the camp entrance fired a couple of shots in the direction of where they believe the sniper had shot our guy from, they probably did not see anyone as the IRA would have scarpered straight away having killed a soldier. The sentry in his post, not far from the unloading bay fired a couple of rounds in the direction of where he believed the sniper was firing from. It was obviously someone shooting from the flats, as they were within walking distance of our position and you could see them from the unloading bay. As such it meant whoever had shot the soldier, had a clear shot.

The sergeant major of the Green Jackets came over to me and told me, 'You did a good job son, well done.' It must have been a good job as I found out later from my best mate in Germany that it had been on orders about me being mentioned in despatches. I didn't even know what that was.

I knew at the time that I wasn't scared. I also thought to myself, I volunteered. Everyone seemed to be congratulating me. I got a bit caught up in the moment as I wasn't in the infantry. I was a signaller, so my reactions were being considered to have been good, like that of a rifleman. I thought they always taught us that you are a soldier first and a tradesman second.

Young John said to me, 'So you weren't scared then Corporal?' I told him at the time I wasn't scared. I think my body was running on adrenalin as I felt every part of my body tingling, almost like the fairy in Peter Pan. It was hard to describe exactly how I felt for the next couple of hours, on a high, on drugs, sort of like sex and drugs at the same time. I thought to myself I never stopped remembering how I felt when the young guy took his last breathe or the sight of the hole in the side of his neck as the blood pumped out for those few seconds. I was worried as I thought at the time it couldn't have been natural to be exhilarated after someone has been shot through the head.

What happened next also stayed with me the rest of my life. John asked what that was. I went on to tell him about that night as I went to bed. It was around midnight when I turned in and I started to think about my life, God and what had happened that day. Like a thunderbolt it came into my head that if I had been just after that rifleman, I would have been the target. It kept going through my mind, as although my twin was schizophrenic and locked up in some asylum, he always talked about God. Me, I had always prayed, although my childhood was full of sadness, pain and awful things, I had always prayed. I prayed when I got caught stealing, I prayed when I did wrong, I prayed when I wanted to join the army, I prayed for everything. Although our childhood was tragic, I always remembered being a little boy and the religious instruction teacher telling me the story of suffer unto me the little children. So although I wasn't a good child I did have a lot of faith and it had seemed to work for me. I started to pray that night. I prayed for the young man who had been shot, I prayed because I couldn't understand what God had planned for me when I had just been in a fifty-fifty situation of life or death. I didn't understand, what had happened that day. It took me a long time to realise what happened that night, especially after I fell asleep.

I told John, 'You are the first person I have told the next part of my story to,' I have often told the story of dragging the

FLASHBACKS

shot man in to the building. I was too embarrassed to tell anyone about the night story. After all that had happened that day, everyone congratulating me, for doing what I believed any soldier would have done.

I had been asleep about two hours when I woke up, I didn't know the time I just knew it was pitch black outside as I could see through the sky lights in the roof of the building. I can only describe my waking up as though I had been given an electric shock, like Frankenstein in the movie. It's as though I had been in a deep sleep and someone had attached electrodes to my body to wake me up. The first thing I realised was that my body was curled up, which was how I went to sleep. But I had awoken and my body as well as being curled up was uncontrollably trembling. Every part of my body from my head to my toes was shaking, like I was a massive jelly on a plate and someone was shaking the plate. The thing was, I was shaking and I thought to myself I will just stop my body shaking by stretching my arms and legs. At least that was my thinking at the time, as I trembled away. I knew what I wanted to do but I could not stop myself from shaking. Then I thought I would shout someone to help me, I went to shout for help, but the only thing that happened was that I couldn't make any noise come out of my mouth. I then went into some sort of nightmare that took me back to the cellar and my father. I remembered when my twin had been thrown down the cellar and I had followed him. I often as a five year old had the same dream and that was being taken from my bed and floating, being dragged without any way of resisting, down the stairs. Whatever it was would collect me and I would float from the bedroom, the

FLASHBACKS

cellar door would open, I would then be dragged into the cellar. At the time I remember thinking the cellar was where evil lived.

Back to the evil I had witnessed that day, I was still trembling for around twenty minutes and then I thought of the only person who had helped me through my life and I prayed for God to help me. I remembered going to sleep praying and I knew what had just happened to my body, did happen, as I remembered being thrown in the cellar as a child. Sure enough my prayers were answered that night and I realised that I had obviously been in shock. I never told anyone about what happened that night because I thought they would think me a coward or weak. So I just put it to the back of my mind, which is where I put things that hurt me, I told John maybe my mind bank overflowed, that could be the reason I ended up in the hospital.

After I told John about that incident, he started to open up a little to me about his own childhood. His parents were druggies and he had been brought up by his grandmother, who he thought the world of. He had only joined the army, to be part of something that his grandmother would be proud of. Sadly young John was not really a soldier in my mind as I didn't believe he could cope with the life, I believed that was the reason he had ended up in hospital. Apparently he had just done a tour of duty where another recruit he had befriended in boy service, killed himself. I reflected back on my time in boy service, there were recruits who could not hack the discipline and believed they had no escape. After the incident John had complained of being tired and unable to do anything. He was perhaps the only soldier in the ward that had very little action

FLASHBACKS

to speak about, however I believe his friend killing himself did not help. I believe he had problems that maybe stretched back to his young childhood as he did confide in me that he was around seven when his real parents pissed off. I thought to myself maybe they did him a favour, but then again, he ended up in hospital so maybe not. I tried after that to take him further under my wing as he wasn't a soldier; he was a young man who wanted to be a soldier, but didn't have the aptitude or fight. He reminded me of my twin and the time he came with me to join the army, but failed to get in. He had similar mannerisms to John, I thought, may be John was schizophrenic.

There was a big difference between John and I, he didn't seem to have any fight in him, whereas I seemed to want to fight everyone and everything. I often wished I could be as laid back as John, but I could see where he was ill, yet I didn't see anything in me that made me believe I was ill. I thought maybe the medication was doing its job for me and then I thought maybe it was up to me to find out what was wrong with me by stopping taking the medication. John and I went back to the ward and that's when I decided to put into action some of my plans regarding my medication. I didn't start straight away; I decided to give the old Colonel an ultimatum to get me out of the hospital.

My next appointment came around to see the Colonel – Colonel Shrink as he was known – as there was a TV program called *Hogan's Heroes* where the camp commander was Colonel Clink, hence the name Colonel Shrink.

I thought the Colonel liked me, as I wasn't aggressive with him and I was sure that he knew I wasn't trying to work my

FLASHBACKS

ticket, as there were a few soldiers on the ward, who were just fed up with the army discipline and wanted to get out. The ones that wanted to get out were in my opinion not good soldiers. Most of them had not seen or done much as soldiers, with regards to action, they just couldn't handle the regime. In the few months I had been in hospital, there were two or three soldiers off the ward, given their marching orders. In retrospect there were also a few soldiers that I thought were really mad or ill, who disappeared off the ward and had apparently gone back to their units, which at the time gave me a bit of hope that I would get back to my unit.

So I went on my appointment with the Colonel. We basically carried on from where we left off. This time I decided I would tell him about my first soldier dying in action, the story I had just told young John. I told him about the first soldier I had seen killed, whilst working as a proper soldier, instead of on exercise. I didn't know until that day, speaking to the Colonel that what I had suffered, the night after the soldier died, was shock. He told me that I should have informed someone, the medical officer or my troop commander, as I should have had some sort of counselling for the incident. I told him, there is no such thing as a soldier. If there were such a thing at the time, half the army would be getting counselling, I told him we did have some sort of counselling, it was called your mates. Basically you would tell a mate a war story, he would probably laugh and then you would get pissed together.

I told him I had never forgot that night as I had never forgot some of my childhood, when my mother's lover stabbed his rival. I learned to live with such things, as I thought everyone

FLASHBACKS

had a similar life. I could not talk about such things as a child, in the same way as a soldier you could not talk about such things, because you felt you would be seen as a wanker or someone who could not hack it. He asked me if I felt like a wanker or in some way inferior that I couldn't talk about my feelings. I said that was not the case and in truth I did not confide in any person, as I believed it would have been a sign of weakness.

I never saw my mother confide in anyone about her own demons, the demons in her life that had seen her struggle through life, with one person after the other who she loved being taken away or killed. Be it her parents, her brother or even Tony, the only man outside her family that I believed she loved. She could do nothing to stop those deaths and she just absorbed them into her mind. In the same way I absorb the bad things that have happened to me. I remember the sadness in my mother's face the day she got the message from the prison that Tony had committed suicide. He left her a note saying that he loved her so much and he could not live without her, especially as he had been in there four months and my mother could not afford to visit him. The fact was that she loved Tony and although she was sleeping with his rival, his rival had a lot of money. In the same way my mother would have slept with a German soldier to save her brother. She would sleep with the man who Tony stabbed, purely because he gave her money to feed her children.

I told the Colonel, 'So you see Sir, in my mind you have to have courage to keep the things that hurt you to yourself. I was told never to feel sorry for myself by my mother. If she could do that with her history, then my shaking in the night, was a very small thing to pay and I believed I had put the memory of that night in to a memory box, to be forgotten.'

He asked me if I had discussed the incident with the other guys when we got drunk.

I told him, 'Only to have a laugh Sir.'

'You had a laugh about a man dying?'

'Not really,' I told him. The incident was brought up when the second soldier on that tour died. The 1st Royal Green Jackets were mainly from south London and as such, there were in that particular battalion a lot of guys from Afro-Caribbean decent, mainly Londoners. One evening, one of the riflemen from the Green Jackets was cleaning his weapon on his bunk. At the same time he was giving the Royal Army medical Corps medic a hard time, stating, as the medic was also of Afro-Caribbean decent, he should have joined a proper regiment like the Green Jackets, instead of becoming a medic. The infantryman was going on and on about medics not being soldiers and that he as an infantryman was far superior in all his soldiering skills. The Colonel of course stood up for the medic and rightly so as I remembered the medic trying to save the life of the guy shot in the head. I remember feeling relief when the medic came over to help me that day. With the medic who was getting grief from the infantryman, in some ways it was funny. I went on to tell the Colonel how the medic got quite upset about the guy giving him a hard time about not being a proper soldier.

'Personally,' I told the Colonel, 'I would rather have had the medic alongside me in action than the infantryman.'

FLASHBACKS

Regiments aside, the medic got so fed up with the ravings of the infantry man that he challenged him to a duel. The duel was that the medic had as his personal weapon, a sub machine gun, known as an SMG. The infantry man had his self-loading rifle, which was the normal weapon of every soldier, except for medics as the SLR was bigger and heavier than the SMG. I believe medics carried the lighter sub machine gun, as they would find it difficult to run with a rifle.

The challenge between the two soldiers was to see who could load their individual weapons the fastest. Loading drills are the same for whatever weapon you are using. You push a magazine on to the weapon, (magazine being the case that holds the bullets). You then pull the working parts back, known as cocking your weapon. Having done those two things, the weapon is loaded. You would then apply the safety catch, unless you are going to fire it straight away. The problems with the SMG, is that when you pull back the working parts, you had to physically pull the cocking handle as it was known all the way back and push it up in to the hooked/locked position. If you do not pull it all the way back to the hooked position, the working parts can slip forward on the massive spring. If that happens and you have a magazine on with bullets in the magazine, the working parts will pull out a bullet from the magazine and fire it.

Sadly the medic was stood about four feet away from the infantryman, facing each other, while another soldier did the timing to see who could load their weapon the faster. The idea was that they would change weapons after the first round and use each other's weapon to load. The overall time for both drills would be added together, which would then decide who the best soldier was. The infantryman started with his own weapon, but sadly never got to use the medic's weapon, although he won his bet, he lost his life.

He won his bet as he had proved he was a better soldier when he was loading his rifle. Being a good soldier, he was pushing on an empty magazine, so there would be no bullets in his weapon. The medic however, without thinking, was rushing to win the bet, without obviously thinking he was pushing on a full magazine of live ammunition. He was rushing to put the magazine into the weapon, which he managed quite quickly, he then went to pull back the working parts to hook the parts back which would have made the weapon ready to fire. But because he was rushing he didn't get the working parts totally hooked back and as such they slipped forward, taking a bullet into the breach. The weapon fired the bullet, entering the infantryman's face, just under his nose. As the two soldiers were about four feet apart, the front of the sub machine gun was only about three feet from the infantryman. You could say he was lucky, in that the weapon was on single shot and not automatic, which would have emptied all the bullets out of the magazine in to the guys face. It turned out it did not need all the bullets as the one that came out, killed him instantly. The Colonel then asked me if I had seen it happen, I said, 'No sir, I saw it a few seconds later as everyone rushed in to find out who had fired the shot.' Typical soldier mentality, a rifleman shouted medic, which made everyone laugh.

At first there was pandemonium as the infantryman who had just been killed was a very popular man in the battalion as

FLASHBACKS

he was one of the battalion's champion boxers. It became apparent that they had to get the medic out of there fast, as the infantryman's mates were going to lynch him. Being a medic, he, like me had just joined the battalion for that tour of duty.

The Colonel came back to what was funny about a soldier dying. I said, 'It's not funny Sir, but soldiers make it funny to deal with it, without looking weak.'

I told him how later on when the lads were getting pissed to deal with what had happened, the soldier who was lying on his bed behind the infantry man said, 'I was reading one of those little war comics with the pictures.'

He was quickly interrupted by another soldier, telling him not to lie as everyone knew he couldn't read and he must have just been looking at the pictures.

The soldier reading the comic then went on to say, 'It was funny as in the comic the hero had just turned and shot some advancing Japanese soldiers, he then said the blood and brains of the killed soldier were all over the comic, he thought that was amazing.

'It wasn't funny but, we made it funny as was the case with every incident like that I had dealt with in the army.'

He said, 'You never spoke to anyone with regards to these incidents?' I then informed the Colonel, that I spoke to the only person I knew that I believed could help me. The person that I knew had been with me all my life and continued to be with me through all my trials and tribulations. I could never confide in a mortal person, as I may have been classed as a nutter.

'Who was that?' the Colonel asked.

'God,' I replied. It was not cushty or good to mention

FLASHBACKS

God; as a soldier you may get ridiculed. I told him that my twin brother was schizophrenic and he did nothing but talk about God. 'I always believed in God and prayed,' I told the Colonel, 'not because I was schizophrenic, but because I had faith and it was real.' I could not prove it to him but I knew in myself, God had always been there for me, I had been in too many near misses not to have someone looking out for me..

The other thing of course was my twin, who was still institutionalised and stuck in some mental home. His God was real to him in a way that only he knew about and I guess I felt the same. I then went on to tell the Colonel about my first meeting with a soldier when I mentioned God. It was in the careers office in Sheffield after I had passed everything for enlistment. The sergeant asked me what religion I was, I told him I believed in God, but I had never been to church. I said If I had a religion, it would be the same as my mothers, as I was proud of my Greek roots. I told the sergeant that I was Greek Orthodox. He laughed and said, 'Well I am going to put you down as Church of England as I can't spell fucking orthodox.' So I became Church of England as far as the army was concerned.

'So you see Sir, I did have someone to confide in, someone in my opinion above any human person, I never got let down in my prayers,' I told the Colonel, I believed there was some irony with the infantry man that died as in some ways he brought it on himself, as the way I saw it. The infantryman was trying to belittle another man, for some sort of self gratification, rather like a bully.

The Colonel then asked, 'Is God with you now and if so where is he? It seems you have been let down. I took in what

FLASHBACKS

he said, thinking the guy must not believe in God.

I told him, 'I didn't understand what was happening to me at that time. I knew I had had problems in my mind when I had seen bad things as a soldier. I would always have a problem when faced with the fact that I would have to kill or be killed, but that was something that I would face when and if I needed to. That was something I never spoke to anyone about, only God.' I said, 'please don't think I am some religious nutter sir, I am only telling you about God and my feelings because I know it to be God that has saved my life on many occasions, when other people have died.'

I told him if I wasn't thinking straight at that time it was because of the medication I was taking. The only thing that crossed my mind a great deal as a soldier was the fact that in the Bible it says if you live by the sword, you will die by the sword. The other thing is that when I joined the army, whilst signing for Queen and country I took the oath on the Bible I was issued. I still have the Bible and at the time I enlisted, I believed it was the right thing to do, as I felt it, when I received the Queen's Shilling and that small Bible.

'The truth is Sir,' I told him, 'I have never discussed my feelings or faith with any soldier up to that day. As I told you before, God and religion are not something you talk about as a soldier. Just because I never mentioned it before, doesn't make it any less real to me. I am not sure what has happened to me, to end up here but I am certain, whatever the outcome, I will still have the faith that I always had. I know it is very difficult, having faith as a soldier, but when I first went to Ireland and saw that young soldier killed, I didn't understand, why he had to die.'

FLASHBACKS

In the same way, I told him about when we'd just arrived in Northern Ireland and you would think as a soldier you have more chance of dying in Northern Ireland than your wife and child at home in England. Yet that is what happened to a young soldier who had just been in Ireland a week when his wife and child were killed in a road accident in England.

'I don't understand about these things,' I told the Colonel, 'but whatever happens, I never lose faith. Please trust me Sir, I can assure you that I am not crazy or a religious nutter. I know something has happened, that has put me in hospital, but I believe if I were sent back to my unit, I would be fine.'

'Right,' was his response, 'let's leave it there for now corporal.' I quickly said, does that mean I can go back to my unit?'

'Afraid not, we need to discuss what happens and treatment' said the Colonel.'

As I left, I was worried as I thought, the Colonel thinks I am crazy or something, I knew I shouldn't have mentioned God or what faith I have, as I was starting to think the Colonel may think I am a religious nutter, or Bible basher. I was nothing of the sort, just a man who had used faith to stay on what I believed, was the right path.

I went to bed that night thinking more and more about my meeting that day with the Colonel. I had to somehow get across that I was genuine; I didn't want to come across like a nutter.

I had never told anyone of importance about the real reason I knew I wasn't a religious Bible basher. My story goes back to the last time I had been injured and had received treatment in the same hospital. I wasn't sure if I should tell the

FLASHBACKS

Colonel my story. I say story, as it may sound a story, but the reality was, it happened for real and it happened to me.

I remembered the night as it was the night I realised I had a guardian angel, the thing that had been with me most of my life. It wasn't until I was in real trouble that, the angel appeared. I was thinking about the incident and I know in my heart of hearts if I tell the truth, I will be ridiculed and maybe thought a nutter. I had been injured and I remembered the last time I was in the hospital, the same hospital that I was now in, I remembered having plastic surgery. It was coming back to me slowly, I could not remember the actual incident, I did remember a couple of soldiers had died. I remember coming in to the hospital and going on leave from the hospital. I remember the leave, as I went on leave looking like the invisible man. My face was covered in bandages and plaster, all you could see of my face was my eyes and my mouth. I remember it well as I ended up shacked up with a gorgeous bird, who thought I was some sort of hero for being a soldier and having had plastic surgery. It was funny because, when I had the bandages removed a few weeks later, she didn't fancy me anymore. Never mind, plenty of fish in the sea as my mother would say.

The serious side of my thoughts went back to the night I had left the hospital. I had been posted to Catterick, where I was an instructor for recruits. I had joined up to serve Queen and country. Being my mother's son, we were brought up to be royalists, to the point that our mother told us that we were related to Prince Philip and the Queen. She would tell us Prince Philip was a cousin. I of course never repeated that to anyone as it was hard enough having faith and not talking about it, for

FLASHBACKS

fear of having the piss taken. I certainly would have been put in a nut house if I told people what my mother had brought me up to believe.

I once again drifted off in my mind, thinking about my first-hand experience of serving Queen and country. I thought back to when I was training recruits at Catterick and the first time I met the Queen. Up to that point I had met or seen many members of the Royal family. The first Royal I met was the Princess Margaret; I say met her I was an eleven year old boy at the time living in South Shields, with an auntie, having been left there by our mother. The other royals were met in the line of duty, Princess Anne and Mark Philips and many others.

All those royals aside, the only true royal in my mind was the one I swore allegiance too. I was thinking how proud my mother would have been, had she been able to see me saying hello to the Queen.

I remembered the Queen fondly after that visit as although I had always thought her a special lady, what she did that day made me realise that she was no fool,. I said you plan for everything on a royal visit and that's what we had done. The one thing you cannot plan for is, of course, the weather. She had just visited us in the bottom of the camp, when it started to piss it down. The Queen is always asked to do something, when on an official visit. The thing she was going to do that day was plant a tree, at the top of the parade square about fifty metres from the headquarters building. The Commanding Officer was escorting Her Majesty, holding an umbrella above her. He kept trying to shield her from the rain. The public were all stood watching and waiting, getting wet

FLASHBACKS

through in the pouring rain. They patiently waited behind a rope barrier, Her Majesty slowly walked towards them. The rope barrier was roped off up to the headquarters building, which was where the Queen was now heading. Her task that day was to take a shovel full of soil out of a barrow and plonk it down on the base of an already planted tree, which would later have a plate saying planted by Her Majesty. You may think doing that was nothing special. However you would be wrong, as the special thing that happened, happened as she was walking up in the rain to do her duty. The dignitaries or people who believed they were more important than the Queen, the officer's wives, the mayor and all his councillors and cronies, basically waited until the Queen started walking up to the planting ceremony. As it was pissing it down, they had stood in the headquarters and only stepped out in to the rain when the Queen was getting closer. We normal soldiers were walking up behind the Queen, we watched as she got nearer to the headquarters. As she got closer the dignitaries slowly made their way out of the building to get wet like the rest of us. The strange thing was that the Queen must have been thinking exactly the same as I was about the so called dignitaries, she did her business with the soil, she did not follow the Colonel's umbrella as he was about to walk up to the quite dry dignitaries. She snubbed the lot of them and went straight over to the public and started chatting to the people she could see had been stood in the rain, awaiting her arrival. The Queen came to my assistance at a later date, so I was right to serve Queen and country. That's how it was with me and many soldiers, Queen first, she wasn't a politician, she gave a toss about every soldier.

FLASHBACKS

To politicians, we were just pawns to be used and abused. Maybe it was because of the Queen's visit that I remembered that night, about the visit from my angel as you do serve God, Queen and country and it has got to be in that order.

I had not been out of hospital that long, having had my face fixed, when I was posted to become an instructor at Catterick. After the Queen's visit I started to seriously think about my position as a soldier. It was mainly because of an incident that resulted in several soldiers dying and I had problems coming to terms with certain things. I could come to terms with the soldiers dying to a degree, but I found it increasingly difficult when I thought about one day, having to kill someone myself. It was as though something had clicked in me when I saw the dignitaries coming out of the building to meet the Queen. I thought they are like politicians; they don't give a toss about anyone, only power. You could tell with the Queen, it was duty. I remember thinking I have always done my duty. I was thinking about the many soldiers I had known who had died, be it from gun battles or even being killed in accidents in the army, which was about the same percentage. I thought I would not be able to go back and fight and kill, but I could not escape, being a soldier. I would have to do my duty, like the many soldiers who had done their duty and died.

I had noticed a pattern to some degree and that was the pattern of life and death, in that in the Bible, it says if you live by the sword, you die by the sword. I was in torment that night for a long time, thinking I wouldn't mind leaving the army, but I could never leave with dishonour and that if I had to die, I would die. I was never afraid to die, I was more afraid to live

FLASHBACKS

with the thoughts of my friends dying and the guilt of surviving when others around me have died. I was more afraid of living with the thought of killing another human being. That would have been something I may not have been able to live with. I still believe I could have justified it with the fact that people were trying to kill me, mainly at that time it was the IRA.

Being a Corporal at the time I had my own space in a bunk room as they call it. So I had my own room. It was around midnight and I had been going through all such thoughts of the day and the army and my life and that of my childhood and my mother's difficult life. I was thinking about the poor policewoman who had been shot outside the Iranian embassy. Basically I was trying to justify my existence as a soldier and such thoughts in some ways gave me the courage to fight and kill if I needed too. Some things seem black and white when it comes to justifiable killing, yet I still was not sure as to whether I wanted to be in that position. I did have some fight in me when I had been in the hospital in London, as it was the time of the Iranian embassy siege. I remember it well as one of the SAS men who entered the embassy ended up in the bed next to me. He had apparently been injured by shrapnel wounds from his own grenade. He had gone through the window too quickly after he had thrown the grenade. I spoke to him for a while and I could see how having to kill someone in his position was acceptable. I believe I would have done the same as he did that day, having seen the poor policewoman murdered.

It was with such thoughts of sadness for the police woman, the soldiers I had known who had died and all their families that I started to think about God and faith. With such thoughts

FLASHBACKS

I was staring out the window at the bottom of my bed and I felt my whole body relax. It was as if my veins had been injected by a calming drug, my heart went to such peace I had never known. I had such love inside me I could not believe, how I could ever feel such peace and love. I was thinking it cannot be happening to me. I just felt so calm.

There were no street lights outside my bunk room, there was no road with car headlights that could reflect, there was nothing outside that bottom floor window but grass and trees about twenty yards away. The first thing I could see looked like a magnet shape, standing on its feet. The magnet shape seemed to light up as I stared in disbelief. The shape formed and as it formed, it looked like it was surrounded in bright stars. I then saw the face of a beautiful young woman, with a white hood, like a shroud over her head and a face which looked like a porcelain doll. Her hands were clasped in prayer and she had her head bowed, it was as though she was looking straight at me. The peace she brought to me that night was real and I know how real it was, as that was the night I believe I was healed, or my torment was healed. The vision, or whatever you want to call it, stayed with me for several minutes, just draining the heartache out of my heart and filling me with love and peace. I could tell the Colonel was thinking I was having delusions but I carried on.

I told him how my body filled with peace and how I watched the lady disappear as the lights started to fade. I jumped out of my bed and went across the corridor to the guy whose bunk room was opposite and told him to come and see. I knew it was real but I needed someone to witness it. He came with me straight away, but all he could see was the darkness. I didn't pursue it that night as I knew if I told him the whole story he would think me crackers. I wasn't crazy and I knew that night was real as after that night, the palms of my hands always would get hot and warm, whenever I was under any sort of duress. It was as though the same warmth that filled my body that night, was now in my hands. I could never tell anyone about that night, but I knew from that night on that I had been blessed by someone, someone who was looking out for me. It was as though my whole life had been mapped out for me and, when it came to the crunch, my life was important.

How is it now that I am waking up back in reality; the reality of my situation is that I am in an army hospital, having had some sort of breakdown. I had never had suicidal thoughts as a child, it must be the medication. I started to doubt my mind that next day, the realisation that I was in an army hospital with only God knowing what was wrong with me. The fact is, whether I am under some sort of sedation or not, even with suicidal thoughts, I know what happened to me that night after the Queen's visit to Catterick was real. I knew because my hands once again became warm. Although reassuring, I had no idea what was going to happen to me. I wasn't about confiding in the Colonel about my visit? I could not bring myself to tell him everything about that night as for sure, he would not understand and as such I was certain, I would have been diagnosed with some sort of schizophrenia. I knew in my heart that the night with the vision was real. With that in mind, I turned to the only thing that I believed could help me and that was prayer. I thought of the lady who came to me that night

FLASHBACKS

long ago and started to pray. Although that night was the first time I had seen anything that made me believe I was watched over and protected, the thoughts of that lady always brought me peace..

I reflected on my childhood, on the near misses I had. Not just in the facts that we could have been buggered at any time by one of the gay lodgers we had living with us. I started to look back as far as I could. The first thing that happened as a child, I remember me and my twin walking across the busy road outside our house. Normally I would always lead and Graham would follow me, as I believed I was the leader of the two of us. We were seven and I remember we were going out to play. Graham ran out in to the road, the next thing was he had been hit by a car. It was not going fast but he ended up with a massive lump in the centre of his head. Maybe it had been that bash on the head that caused his mental illness.

I thought about all the things I had done when my parents split up. I became the feeder of the family. I was such a thief. I never stopped stealing food and anything my mother could sell to earn some money. On reflection I was so lucky never to get caught by the police as you couldn't get in the army if you had been in trouble with the police. Far more dangerous for me was the fact I could have been taken by gypsies or anyone who want to harm me.

I came closest to death in my eyes when I was around eleven. I was still only the size of your average nine year old when I was eleven. There was a large fair that used to come to Rotherham every year. The fairground people, mainly gypsies, would park all their trucks at the side of a brick wall that

FLASHBACKS

separated the fairground-come-car-park, from the River Don that ran alongside. The wall was about five feet high and stretched around four hundred yards. The travellers would park their trucks with the side of the lorry running down the wall. Being an opportunist and hungry, one night I climbed onto the wall and started walking down it, trying the side doors of the trucks as I walked along. Apart from the odd growl of a mad dog, it seemed quite safe. I found a lorry open and as I got inside, I found boxes and boxes of Westler Hamburgers. There were around thirty hamburgers in a tin. I managed to get around six tins, wrapped them in some sack and carried them over my shoulder like Dick Whittington. I managed to get them home to my mother and as such we ate quite well that night, as my mother only had to buy a loaf of bread. Being my mother she congratulated me on my haul, whilst my elder brother, tried to turn me in. My mother told him to leave me alone, slapped him around the face and told him in no uncertain terms that, he didn't mind eating what I had stolen.

The next night I decided to go back, I was not going back for more hamburgers as by then it had occurred to me that there might be money. After carrying on from where I left off the other night, I carried on trying the doors on each lorry as I walked along the wall. It was not long before I struck what I thought was gold. It was a lorry full of slot machines, the types you would put a penny in. I was snooping around when I stumbled on a holdall full of pennies. I thought I had won the jackpot, but being about five stone wet through, I wasn't that strong. Instead of filling my pockets, I had decided to take the whole bag. I couldn't pick it up, so I started dragging it towards the door I had left open, next to the wall. I must have been making too much noise, as I shit myself when the door opposite the one I had opened, suddenly slid open. A scar faced, tattoo infested gypsy opened the door and looked me straight in the eyes. His were full of, I am going to rip your throat and mine must have been full of, shit myself.

He said, 'Come here you little bastard, I am going to skin you alive.' He wasn't exactly fit, which was lucky for me. I jumped over the wall and ran down to the river.

I could hear everyone shouting, 'Catch the little bastard.' I had no alternative but to jump in the river and swim across the river to make my escape as I could hear people and dogs. I am pretty sure I would have disappeared that night had I been caught. The police might have been a better option than a load of irate gypsies.

Another near miss in the thieving games I was playing in those days. By far the greatest triumph I had in the thieving stakes was when I was around twelve years old. I noticed a Chinese restaurant on the main road where we lived had closed. I looked through the window and it seemed deserted so I cased the joint for want of a better word. I noticed looking through the window there was a cigarette machine on the wall with, cigarettes still visible through the glass partitions. I went around the back, broke a window and climbed in. I went down the stairs in to the restaurant and proceeded to break the glass on the cigarette machine. I got all the Senior Service and Park Drive cigarettes out, leaving the Woodbine and Players; I thought I will come back for them later. I got home to my mother with the cigarettes and she gave me five shilling for the lot. She said she had to sell them to make some money. I didn't care as I would do anything for my mother. She asked if there was any money in the cigarette machine. I said I didn't know but was going to find out.

I went back the next night and got all the other cigarettes out, but no money. As I had just climbed out of the window to get out of the place, I was scrambling up a bank to get out of the yard when a guy appeared from the driving school which was next door. I had put all the cigarettes in my shirt and kept them hidden. He shouted, you better clear off young man this place was broken into last night and the police are watching it. Hence I never went back, but once again I had a near miss, so there must be someone watching over me. Of course it never crossed my mind that what I was doing was wrong. Then I justified it in the fact that I never stole for myself, it was always to help my mother get through life, or just feed us. I thought whatever I did as a child, I always remembered to pray.

With all the thoughts of my childhood and life running through my mind, I was sure whatever I was suffering from had come from being a soldier. If my guardian angel had not wanted me to become a soldier, I thought I would have got caught as a child, which would have stopped me becoming a soldier in the first place.

Weeks were turning into months in the hospital, although I had no idea of time as the drugs seem to numb your mind. It seemed I just spent most of the day thinking about going to bed at night.

When my next appointment came around with the Colonel, I had my suspicions that he was a civilian shrink put into uniform to enable him to get some respect from soldiers. Having thought about it, the Colonel didn't appear until after Rifleman T had thrown the table through the window with the young shrink, who was for sure a civilian as after the incident with the rifleman, he disappeared. I think he had no credibility with soldiers. It's as though if you are not in uniform, a soldier doesn't have to listen to you.

My appointment with the Colonel started with him telling me that he had been through my file and he started asking me about an incident when I apparently refused to fly back from a NATO exercise in Denmark. I was attached to the RAF at the time, so you would have thought me happy to fly. I remembered the exercise well as being attached to the RAF was great as the food was better and we could get away with a lot as the RAF didn't have the same discipline. On that exercise we had an Australian SAS captain attached to our unit, he was on exchange, so some lucky bastard had got six months in Oz. He was a good guy as, although he was a Captain, he would have a laugh with us, even to the extent of us calling him Bruce. He would always say, 'Good day mate,' which did seem strange to us as our officers would not have talked to us that way.

I was known as a man who could get anything when I was in the army, my childhood thieving probably helped. My boss was a man we called Captain Jack, a good guy who had risen up through the ranks, so although a normal captain was around thirty, Captain Jack was forty seven and had been in the Army 30 years, so he knew the score. We had been playing soldiers on that exercise for about three weeks, as it was a NATO exercise, my job at the time with the squadron was as a

FLASHBACKS

Forward Air Controller. As there wasn't a lot happening on the air strikes side of things, I had more or less become Captain Jack's and the Aussie Captain's Batman, i.e. I was running them all over the place. Captain Jack trusted me as I think I reminded him a bit of himself as a young Lance Corporal as I was at the time. I was always a cheeky twat, but I was good at my job, so I got away with a lot. Captain Jack was in charge of us and being attached to the RAF we were sort of left alone to do our own thing.

Because it was an RAF exercise, the RAF big boss Air Vice Marshall something or other was coming to inspect us all in the field. Captain Jack told me, 'I know you are good at getting things done Corporal, so as we have the Air Vice Marshall coming, we will have to feed him and basically look after him for the afternoon.' He said, 'I don't think it would be right to

NATO exercise in Denmark. Ground to Air shooting range.

feed him like the rest of us, i.e. eating rations out of our mess tins. The tins were about six by four inches, with a handle and if your food wasn't cold to begin with it was cold as soon as you put it in the mess tins. I was tasked with sorting a suitable tent out that the Air Chief could go in, sit down and have a meal with the main officers on the exercise, so he would be able to say how jolly good everyone was.

I set off with my Land Rover. I knew exactly where I would go as earlier on in the exercise, I had been in to a Danish RAF base in Tirstrup. It was a Danish air base, come army camp. I had been there to drop Captain Jack and the Aussie off at the Officers mess for some sort of do with the Danish Officers.

I arrived at the base and told the soldier in the guardroom that I was on a mercy mission and I had to go to the Officer's

Me shooting at the target.

FLASHBACKS

mess. It wouldn't have happened in England, but because most of the Danes were nice people and spoke English he just asked me if I knew where it was. I said yes. With that I went on to the Officer's mess. Officers' messes are the same whether you are British, Danish or American. They always have non-commissioned officers, looking after them. Tirstrup was no different. They had an old sergeant in charge of the mess. I went up to him and told him that we had Margaret Thatcher coming to visit us in the field in the next couple of days and as she was the Prime Minister we needed to cater for her a little better than a normal visitor. I started to deal with the sergeant and we agreed that if he loaned me what I needed I would give him my jump boots that he had taken a fancy too. I would also get him a bottle of whisky and a beret. He then took me into the officers mess stores, for want of a better word. I came out with, white table clothes, nice plates, wine glasses and wine, cutlery, napkins basically everything you would find in a restaurant. But by far the thing that topped it all was a pair of silver candle sticks complete with candles.

I laughed as I was sure to get plenty of smarty points for that days bit of work. I managed to also borrow some nice tables and chairs from the guy in the sergeant's mess and a paGoda of course. He too wanted a jumper and beret as it appeared those two guys were my equivalent as they negotiated. So I thought I have got a spare pair of boots, a jumper and beret, I will tell Captain Jack and he will sign me a chit to have them replaced. I loaded the stuff into the back of my Land Rover and ended up tying the table and chairs on to the roof of the Land Rover. I then set off back to the wood we were set up in, which as per normal was in the middle of nowhere. We always camouflaged our vehicles and any equipment when we were playing soldiers, as if it were real. On my return, Captain Jack came over, he said he could see the table and chairs and asked if I had managed any plates, I said, 'Yes sir.'

He said, 'Look Corporal I want you to set something up in the wood tonight night as the Air Marshal is coming tomorrow.' He wouldn't have chance to see what I had done as he was busy, so he told me not to let the side down and try my best to make it look presentable.

I went to bed that night thinking it was too late to do anything now, so I just got my head down and waited until first light. At first light, I found a bit of a clearing that I could drive into, then unloaded the furniture and placed the table and chairs behind the Land Rover. I then put up the paGoda above the table and chairs, so I had got myself a nice little dining room. I pulled the camouflage netting over both the Land Rover and the paGoda and got myself loads of bushes and tree branches. I did a good job camouflaging the lot, leaving just a slit as the entrance to my dining room. I then took out all my supplies and after I had finished setting the table up with my engraved plates and cutlery, I placed the candle sticks in the centre of the table and lit the candles. The whole thing looked like something from the Phantom of the Opera. By the time I had finished it was breakfast time, so I made my way over to the cookhouse to have a word with the guys in charge of the field kitchen. They knew they were feeding the Air Marshal but they didn't know where, so I showed them and arranged for them to have the food delivered before the Air Marshal arrived.

FLASHBACKS

I then went and found Captain Jack.

I said, 'I am ready Sir, I have sorted the place out for the Air Marshal to eat.'

He came along with me to my Land Rover and its extension. I opened the netting entrance and as soon as Captain Jack walked in and saw my efforts he just burst into laughter. He said, 'Only you Corporal, I knew you would not let me down.'

He said, 'I am not going to take your thunder for this. I want you to be at the meal with the Air Marshal and tell him yourself how you managed this lot.'

The Air Marshal sure enough arrived and went on his visit around the troops scattered all around the place. Whilst he was doing that I was having all the food placed in the tureens and bowls that I had borrowed from the Danish Air Force. I awaited the arrival of Captain Jack and the Air Marshal and along they came. I saluted and said, 'This way Sir.' Jack had a smirk on his face and as the Air Marshall walked in to the officer's mess in the field I had created, he too burst out laughing. It was like something out of a *Carry On* film.

The Air Marshal turned to my boss and asked him how he managed such a spread.

My boss looked at me and told the Air Marshall, the reason we have Corporal Willey to dine with us, was to explain that very thing Sir.'

The Air Marshal turned to me and said, 'You have done very well Corporal but how did you manage it?'

I then started to tell him how I went to the Danish Air Force base at Tirstrup and managed to chat up the guard commander by giving him my beret to let me in the camp. I told him that we were having a visit from the Prime Minister, i.e. Margaret Thatcher. I said, 'Of course you are more important than the Prime Minister Sir, but I knew they would have heard of Margaret Thatcher.'

'Of course,' he said laughing and asked what happened next.

I said, 'I went to the Officers Mess and spoke to the Mess Sergeant. I told him the same story of Margaret Thatcher. He was impressed and wanted to help, he was more interested in my equipment and I gave him a jumper, a pair of jump boots and a para smock, oh and a bottle of whisky sir. He gave me all the equipment for the dining table. I then saw a mate of the sergeants who I negotiated with and he settled for a beret and a jumper. Of course I had to put up the ante to get something out of it for myself.'

The Air Marshal turned to Capt. Jack and said, 'Ensure the Corporal gets all the equipment replaced that he has given for us to dine out.

I said, 'Thank you Sir.'

The Colonel Shrink enjoyed my story about Margaret Thatcher but he wanted to know why that exercise had caused me to refuse to fly. I told him that that was the first exercise I had done where I had been informed that I had to fly back to England in an RAF Hercules plane. As I was due to go to Northern Ireland again, the thought had not entered my mind about not flying until they told me I had to fly back to England. We had driven to Denmark, having been ferried across the Channel to Germany by troop carrying ships, I then drove to

FLASHBACKS

Denmark. I had not given any inclination that I was by then afraid to fly, I just had a panic attack when I was told. I was going to be driving down to an RAF base in Germany where I would be getting on a Hercules transport plane.

I went and saw Captain Jack and said, 'I cannot get on that Hercules Sir.'

He told me not to be stupid and that I had to get on the plane. He said 'Corporal, I am ordering you to get on that Hercules and do your duty.' I told him I would always do my duty, but I couldn't get on that Hercules. He said he was very disappointed in me but he couldn't help me, if I was refusing an order. I went on to tell Jack why I wouldn't get on the plane. He knew about the incident and arranged for me to drive back to England and we would deal with the incident when we got back to England at the end of the exercise.

I was only being flown back early so I could have some leave before I went to Northern Ireland. The shrink asked me what had happened and what I had told Captain Jack about my reasons for not flying. I started to tell the shrink. I was never keen to fly. That was one of the reasons I wanted to do a parachute course as I thought I would at least be able to jump out of a plane if I had a parachute rather than stay in a plane that might crash. The first time I became a little rattled about flying for real was when I was attached to the RAF in Malta. I was to be stationed in a little place called Luqa. It was a small RAF air field in Malta and my job was to be a Forward Air Controller. It was 1975 and some bloke called Mintoff was the leader or main man in Malta. He had decided he didn't want Malta to remain in the commonwealth and as such he was after independence. My job was to be one of two soldiers attached to the RAF in Malta and as well as operating the communications with the RAF Harriers, I would also be helping out with the Sea Harriers as Malta was being closed down as far as we British were concerned. I think we were showing a bit of power on our way out. As such we had HMS Hermes in the harbour at Valletta, the capital of Malta.

On the Hermes were 42 Commando, the Royal Marines. It was going to take around six weeks for the handover, so there were planes flying in and out of RAF Luqa daily. Whilst I was never a keen flyer, it would never have stopped me doing my duty. After about two weeks into the handover of Malta I was doing my normal job, playing soldiers and Forward Air Controlling. I was quite laid back about it, as being attached to the RAF was such a doddle in comparison to when I was with an Infantry battalion or Artillery or any other army unit where you always got bullshit. The RAF were different, everyone was so laid back. The equivalent of the infantry in the RAF was the RAF Regiment and even they were not as bullshitty.

The RAF Regiment's main job with the RAF was to guard bases and runways, so they were always about. As life could be quite boring for them they would always have a laugh somewhere. I remembered them in Belize; six of them had made one foot square signs, they would have two each, one in each hand. They wrote 5.0 or 5.5 or 6.0 on the signs and as there were RAF planes flying in and out of Belize with troops and supplies nearly every day, they would stand at the side of the runway and await a plane coming in, they would hold the cards up so the pilot could see his marks for landing and taking

FLASHBACKS

HMS Hermes

off. It was the same guys I had been out in Belize with that were now doing the same thing in Malta. Service men in general will always find a way of having a laugh and that was their way.

The Colonel interrupted me and said that is all very interesting corporal but could you get to the point, with regards to not wanting to fly. I apologised and told him I was trying to get to the point. I went on to explain about the fact that they had many planes in Malta that they would refuel in mid air. The plane the RAF used for refuelling planes was called a Vulcan; a massive plane that basically looked like a flying triangle with a front cockpit on it. It was all wings, which is where I believe all the fuel was stored and a long pipe with a nozzle on the end would be released out of the back of the Vulcan. The idea was that the plane that required refuelling would fly beneath the Vulcan and attach itself to the nozzle. Not something I would

FLASHBACKS

have fancied as I could imagine it might be a little dangerous.

Well I found out how it could be dangerous to fly a Vulcan after having only been in Malta for a few weeks. We were actually based a few hundred yards away from the runway and as such were very close to the planes landing and taking off. I was relaxing and sunbathing outside my tent when I first heard and then saw the massive Vulcan bomber, flying over my head, heading out to sea. I thought it must have over shot the runway as I was sure it was the same Vulcan I had just watched coming in to land. I remember landing in the Hercules a few weeks prior and the Loadmaster or Engineer on the plane told us about the runway at Luqa being a bit dodgy as planes sometimes over shot the runway because the runway had a massive dip in it, so you needed to get your approach just right so you didn't hit the dip.

As the field we were camped in, was just at the end of the runway, you could see the planes coming in to land and taking off, they would disappear into the dip in the runway. You would then hear the reverse thrust of the engines as the plane reappeared out of the dip. I was just sat reading something and was disturbed by a loud engine noise, I looked up to see a massive Vulcan plane coming in to land. I saw it disappear into the dip and then it sounded like the reverse thrust had been engaged. The thing I did notice was the noise as it landed, I believed it was the reverse thrust but there was also quite a bang. Then I heard the louder noise of the engines as the plane revved up to go around again. As I was to find out later the pilot had messed up the landing and because of that had decided to go around again. It once again flew over my head

FLASHBACKS

and it started heading out to sea. I watched as the plane banked left again, heading across my line of sight, like I was sat in the movies. I thought there was something wrong when I saw smoke coming out of the engines.' I carried on watching the plane, thinking that things didn't look good. Then the whole plane exploded in a massive ball of fire. I watched it disintegrate, some parts went in the sea and other parts looked like they were hitting land. I thought no one could have survived; I am still not sure to this day how anyone survived, but apparently some parachuted to safety. I did not see the parachutes as I was watching the ball of flame as it exploded. The Colonel asked me if I told anyone what I had witnessed, I said I didn't tell anyone important what I had seen. I was going to tell the powers that be what I had seen after the news came through to everyone that the Vulcan had blown up.

Some duty RAF Officer had arrived from RAF Luqa, he wanted to know about anyone who had seen what had happened. Prior to me opening my mouth to say what I had seen, the Officer told us from what they understood the aircraft had come in to land at Luqa and the pilot had maybe not judged the dip too well in the runway. As such he had landed too heavy and believing the under carriage may have been damaged, he decided to take off and go around again, which turned out to be a big mistake. It turned out that the RAF believed he had come in so heavy he somehow punctured the fuselage. The wheels, I believe, hit so hard that they rammed upwards, into the fuselage. That's what he told us anyhow. I was about to put my hand up to say I saw what happened when he said there would have to be a court of enquiry into

FLASHBACKS

RAF Vulcan Bomber, similar to the one I saw explode in Malta.

the crash. A Corporal out of the RAF who was stood at my side when the Officer was speaking told me that if you see an accident like that you would probably get flown back out to Malta as a witness. Having just seen a plane explode, the last thing I thought I would want to do is get on a plane to fly out to Malta again, so I said nothing.

I didn't feel too great the next couple of days in Malta, I know it was probably shock but even then I didn't know about such things. The only thing I knew to do when something like that happens was what I always did, get drunk.

My mate was an aircraftman, which is basically a private in the RAF. His name was Plug; as he had teeth that resembled bugs bunny he was christened *Plug*. Although I had been initially christened *prick* when I joined the army, I was now known as *Greco*, because of my mother's background.

FLASHBACKS

Plug and I had decided to go to Selima, which was a bit up the coast from us. As we had all day, we decided to work our way along the front, having a drink in every bar we came across. As Selima stretched for a couple of miles on the front, there were about three hundred bars, so we decided to remain in a bar that had made us welcome. Of course by then we were pissed. Plug decided he would go back to camp as he had had enough. I had other ideas; I decided to get the open air bus to Valetta, the capital.

I had been working with the marines from 42 Commando in the past so I knew a couple of them quite well. I knew the aircraft carrier was still docked in the bay in Valletta, so that was my thinking at the time. I headed into the city and down to the gut, as it was known, the gut being basically a long lane that ran parallel with the main road through Valetta. It was situated about one hundred yards downhill from the main road. The gut in Malta was famous for all the brothels and bars that were there mainly to entertain all the sailors that would arrive in Malta. I knew if there was a brothel down there I was likely to bump into my mate Chris (we became good mates whilst in Belize). I was by then staggering my way along the road, I didn't manage to get far down before I was tempted into a brothel. I had my way with a gorgeous Maltese bird; well I thought she was Maltese, she could have been anything as the only English she spoke was, how much and thank you. I left that bar and was working my way down the gut when I came across a few commandos in a bar. I asked if any of them knew Chris and they said they did and he was out on the town that night as they had come ashore with him. The only thing I could do was look for him. As I had not seen him for over a year, it would be a great piss up, not that I wasn't pissed already. I was wandering the gut looking for my mate, remembering how we met and became mates. We were both Forward Air Controllers in Belize. He did the same job as me for the marines and I was the man on the ground for the army. We had ended up in the jungle together, he was operating the Harriers off the Ark Royal and I was doing the same with the RAF Harriers situated in Belize.

In the jungle we became good mates as he was half Hungarian and I was half Greek. Being in Malta brought back the memories of Chris and I going to a brothel in Belize. The hotel was in the middle of nowhere, a place called Punta Gorda. We had been playing soldiers in the middle of the jungle near the Guatemalan border. Our main job there was to provide communications for the Special Air Service and of course the Special Boat Service, the Navy equivalent to the SAS. We didn't really understand the politics of the situation, only that Edward Heath the Prime Minister at the time had sent us there. After about six weeks of roughing it in the jungle, the powers that be, decided we deserved a break. They had booked us into the nearest hotel, which also happened to be quite posh. It was called the Pelican Beach for obvious reasons, there were pelicans there and it was on the beach. It was the main base for lots of rich tourists and divers, as there was a great deal of interest in that part of the world.

At that time the Calypso, which was the boat owned by Jacques Cousteau, a famous sea explorer and diver, was moored off the coast. A lot of the rich people staying at the Pelican

FLASHBACKS

Beach were divers or film crew from the show that Jacques Cousteau was making at the time. That part of the Barrier Reef off Central America was famous for sharks, mainly hammer heads. As me and Chris had been in the jungle from the beginning of the conflict we were due some respite and that's where they booked us in as it was cheaper to keep us down the coast than fly us back and forth in the Wessex helicopter, they used at the time to ferry us around the jungle.

It was one of the best times in my Army career, meeting up with Chris, as we were both of the same mentality, that being mad as hatters. We couldn't believe our luck when they put us in that hotel, we were not sure how long we would be there, only that we had the weekend off and we would also have the use of a Land Rover that had been left there. I believe it belonged to the SAS or the infantry blokes who were doing jungle warfare training. We weren't bothered about when we were going back to the jungle as we were just going to make the most of our time. Having been in the jungle weeks, we stunk, so the first thing we did was to get washed up and washed our kit. It dried in no time and we were off then, to find the local bars. We had just left the hotel and we came across a local in the middle of the road who could not speak. I don't know what happened to him, but the only communication he could make was a grunt which sounded like a butbut noise, like a stammer, so we called him *But But*. He gave us a sign with his fingers to his mouth, asking us if we wanted a smoke. So we offered him a cigarette. He waved no and beckoned us to follow him, as he gave us the sign for a smoke and the sign, by waving his hands from shoulder to bum of a woman and the sign off a drink, putting his right hand up to his mouth. So we decided to go with him as he was obviously local and he knew where to go, for everything we wanted.

As we were walking, we got quite attached to But But. Although he could not talk he was funny, behaving like a jester as we walked along the road. We had gone about half a mile when he stopped us and beckoned us in to a small clearing in the middle of the jungle. We were a little apprehensive as there had been soldiers murdered in Belize, but not down where we were. We thought But But wouldn't be capable of taking me and Chris on, so we just followed him. After about a hundred yards down another track, we found what he wanted to show us. He had his own little business going in the middle of nowhere – he was growing marijuana. He must have had about two hundred plants. We guessed then that But But was the main man for the rich tourists in the Pelican Beach. He didn't know we were servicemen and we decided not to say anything, rather decided to let him think we were tourists. We then gave him the thumbs up and asked him where we could find a bar and women. He once again gave us the follow me sign and off we went with But But.

He was such a funny guy, very friendly as we didn't make fun of him stuttering to talk or the way he walked, which was also strange, we just went along with him. After about a mile walk, we ended up in a small village, apparently it was where But But lived. We walked up what seemed the only road in the village and stopped outside a hut, the hut was the village bar. The only drink they had was called one barrel as it was known, a sort of brandy, we had drunk it before in Belize. You had one

FLASHBACKS

barrel, two barrel, three barrel and depending how pissed you wanted to get, decided which one you chose. One of the guys reckoned someone told him that they had started a generator with the three barrel. So when you drank it you watered it down with coke or lemonade, I mean about a quarter of an inch of spirit in the bottom of a glass would be plenty and you would then dilute with lots of coke or lemonade.

Me and Chris started having a drink with But But, then he brought out the joints, as I had never had marijuana I thought I will give it a whirl. Chris was in his element as he had had loads of the stuff as he had been in Central America before. I had smoked half a joint and I could not understand what the fuss was about smoking marijuana, as all it did for me was make me feel relaxed. I was relaxed when But But told us to follow him and took us with our drinks and joints in to another hut, where we found our choice of young women. Being both pissed and stupid we decided to shag them, that's when I noticed the benefit of marijuana. Had we not been high we may have been a little smarter and thought about the consequences of shagging a local in the middle of the Central American jungle; we could have caught anything. More luck than judgement, we got away with it, we gave But But ten Belizean dollars each and he was happy, I think it was about three pounds in English. We went back to the hotel that night and we were both too zapped out to notice all the talent that was staying in that hotel.

That was until the next day, we woke up in wonderland, as far as we were concerned. We had our man pack radios for communications, the equivalent of mobile phones. There was

FLASHBACKS

the military Land Rover that had been left there, which we had the use off. We got in touch with our superiors and we were told they didn't believe the conflict was going to escalate. As such we were to stay in the hotel until further notice. We were told to carry on working, rather than living in the jungle, we could stay in the hotel at night. During the day, we were to drive as far as we could into the jungle, leave the vehicle and trek into the jungle to meet up with the SAS for a briefing. That was going to start on the Monday and as it was Saturday, Chris and I decided we should once again, go and find But But, to sort out some weed and women.

We decided between us and But But, we didn't want to be going back to his village and the jungle hut we had been in the day before. Instead we would rather take the women back to our hotel to have a bit more luxury. But But waved no, he made out the local women were not allowed in the hotel unless they worked in the kitchens or gardens. We carried on pestering him and told him we would give him more money. In the end he went along with us and fixed us up with two more women. We all jumped in the land rover and headed back to the hotel. As soon as we got there, the girl I was with refused to go in to the hotel and even with But But giving her grief she would not budge. The woman who was with Chris decided she would still come into the hotel, so we sneaked her in and Chris had sex. I was more or less falling asleep listening to him having sex with his jungle bunny, which is what we had christened them. He then pointed at me and said, 'can my mate have sex with you now'. I wasn't bothered to be quite honest as I was stoned and drunk in any case. But it was funny as she jumped up and

FLASHBACKS

grabbed her clothes and shouted, in her best Caribbean dialect, 'No way two'.

I burst out laughing and she ran to the door to run away. She was running down the corridor half naked and I shouted in my best WC Fields voice, 'Come here my little Fillie.'

Chris and I were both stoned, but we had to help the poor girl get out of the hotel, which we did. Unfortunately we did get caught by the owner and he told us in no uncertain terms that we were out of order. We apologised and said it would not happen again, as we didn't realise it was not allowed.

The next day Chris and I had breakfast and decided to get our kit ready as we would be driving out to the jungle, the next day, so we spent most of the morning cleaning our weapons and sorting the radio equipment out. Then we decided we would check out the hotel for dinner as we had been living off marijuana and But But the first couple of days. Most of the guests at the hotel were rich divers. They were intrigued to say the least as to who we were and what we were doing. Chris being a marine had done quite a lot of diving and could talk about it. As we were talking to a couple of rich women, who were also fit, I was waiting for him to start talking about diving. No, he comes out with some great bull shit. He tells everyone we are pilots and said he was surprised that they had not seen us flying up and down, doing sorties along the coast. When they asked why we were staying in a hotel, he just said that it was a mixture of rest and recuperation. He went on to say, we were working with Special Forces in the jungle, providing them with air strikes as and when they needed them.

FLASHBACKS

Although the SAS were in the jungle and we had met up with them, I wondered what he was going to say next. He then came out with a pearl, he blurts out we would be flying up and down next week and we could buzz the hotel on our way back to the Ark Royal. One off the woman then said she had seen the ship on her way to the Pelican Beach. She had been diving off the Quays, the little islands that were between Central America and Florida. With that they said they would look out for us, I wasn't sure if they believed him or not but I couldn't stop laughing when they walked away.

Chris said, 'Trust me mate we will be shagging them soon.'

I said, 'We may be a bit out of our depth.' The next day we had our orders and set off to meet up in the jungle with the SAS patrol. The patrol we met up with were planning to recce one of the Guatemalan positions.

The real worry about the Guatemalans was that as they were neighbours of Cuba and also situated next to Belize. The worry was that, if the Guatemalans invaded Belize, the Cubans could then take over Guatemala and then the whole of Central America would be communist. The truth was that there wasn't much chance of Guatemala doing anything as the reconnaissance by the SAS showed that their Air Force consisted of a Dakota DC3 and a few bi-planes. That was probably why we had been stepped down a bit having been in the jungle for six weeks. The map reference we had where we would be meeting the patrol was about twenty miles away from where we were staying. We could get about three miles from the place with the Land Rover and then we would have to trek, which was nothing that we were not used to.

FLASHBACKS

When we arrived at the map reference point, it turned out to be some sort of pond, like a hole in the middle of the jungle, it was known as the Blue Hole. We found out later from the patrol that the hole was known as the Blue Hole and that it was supposedly famous. According to them it was one of the wonders of the Caribbean, if not the world. I remembered someone in the hotel had been talking about it and were contemplating diving in it. Apparently quite a few divers had gone in at that point and disappeared. We were sat at the side of it, looking down into the water, when I saw a snake swimming across the top. I thought, not for me. That aside it had taken us a few hours to get to the position as we had to trek with our weapons and radio equipment. When we met up with the patrol, we were told that they wanted an air strike and gave us the coordinates for the attack. It was our job to pass on the coordinates for the attacks to the Harrier pilots. Of course they were real coordinates and the Harriers did come in very low, but they did not fire anything as this was all practice in case they had to do it for real. Nevertheless the attacks themselves seemed real, especially at night as the attacks were always based on your own position so they would come in to do a sortie, maybe two hundred yards away from where you were.

I remembered the first attack when we had just arrived in the jungle and called up an air strike. Within a few minutes there was a Harrier hovering above our heads and the noise at night was deafening, albeit very exciting. None of us believed that it was going to kick off for real as the Guats really had nothing like our forces and if the Cubans gave any grief the Yanks would have been straight in with us. Still it was good fun

FLASHBACKS

and real soldiering for a while. Now we were informed that the British were watering down the amount of air strikes as it seemed that a political solution was on its way, so we were just practicing and keeping the Guats on their toes by the odd sortie to show them we were still here.

Brilliant is what me and Chris thought, but the truth was we did deserve it having been in the jungle for six weeks without a break. We were going to make the most of our semi working break. That afternoon as normal we were given the coordinates for the Harriers target and as the Harriers would come in and do their bombing run they would then fly off over the sea, either flying back to the Ark Royal if they were Sea Harriers or up the coast to Airport Camp in Belize city. We gave the pilots the coordinates, which brought them within a few hundred yards of our Blue Hole, which is quite visible so they probably didn't need coordinates to hit that target, we also gave them the coordinates of our hotel which they had to pass on their way back.

I am sure the pilots were more than happy to zap our hotel as it involved them flying up the coast instead of over the jungle. Our plan was pretty fool proof as the only person besides us, who knew about the practice, would be the pilots and they would just think it another sortie on the way back. They couldn't miss our hotel anyway as it had Pelican Beach in massive writing on the roof as most of the people staying there would arrive by boat or being rich a lot arrived by helicopter, which in truth was the best way in to the jungle.

The barrier reef, which was in fact the second biggest barrier reef in the world, was about half a mile from the hotel and that's where a lot of the divers went to dive, plus of course to rub shoulders with Jacques Cousteau, who at that time, had been filming there for months. About an hour after the Harriers had done their sortie in the jungle, the leader of the SAS patrol asked to meet up with us at noon on Wednesday, giving us a day off.

We arrived back in the hotel in the early evening and got ourselves cleaned up. Although we had no civilian clothes, we had jungle shirts and decent lightweight trousers that had been nicely washed and ironed by the maid. So we didn't smell and looked quite casual. We went down to dinner and the two women we had been speaking to the day before, came up to us and said, 'We wondered how long it would take you to get back.'

They had seen us coming back in the hotel with our radio equipment that was nicely packed away in our bergans or ruck sacks. They asked us if they could join us for dinner, of course we did not object.

They had only been sat down a second when the one which was to become mine said, 'We saw you today and you were amazing.' Apparently we, or the real pilots, had come in and done the bombing run, they had roared in about fifty feet above the hotel and scared everyone on the beach, which was where the girls had been when the aircraft did their bombing run. They said we were great, we couldn't believe our luck, as not only did they ask us if we were working the next day, but we ended up shacking up with them that night. Money was a problem as we had very little and although our food was covered, everything else wasn't. I left that one to Chris as well.

FLASHBACKS

He told them we were not allowed to have money on us, or anything else that may identify us in case we had to ditch.

The girls, as they later became known to me and Chris, said that money wasn't a problem to them and insisted we put our drinks on their account, as their parents would be settling the bills. We then proceeded to get merry together and Chris took one of the girls back to our room and I went back with Liz as she was known to her room. After a great night of passion and thinking I was James Bond, the four of us got together for breakfast. As we had the day off the girls asked us if we wanted to spend the day with them. Of course we didn't have a mission that day so we decided to go with the girls. They had hired a motor boat and at the same time got us some diving equipment.

We all set out to the Barrier Reef, the girls were quite experienced, not only at sex, but apparently they were both divers. I of course said I had had a go at diving but was more into playing around with a mask and flippers. Chris was a qualified diver, being a Marine it was second nature to him. Chris and his girl, Bee as she was known, went out over the Barrier Reef to dive where all the hammer heads and other sharks were swimming. Me and Liz decided to just snorkel on the reef side nearest to the coast, which she informed me had no big sharks. Of course after we had dropped Bee and Chris in the sea, we knew they had an hour of diving so I practiced my diving in the boat and had sex for forty minutes before having a ten minute snorkel.

We went back and picked up Chris and Bee who were full of their shark encounters. We headed back to the beach to chill out, only to bump into But But. He came up to us and grinned at me and Chris, we said hello to him and he sort of spoke back the best he could. Liz and Bee asked who he was and how we knew him, so we told them about But But and how he looked after himself by growing his own marijuana. Being of a certain age the girls were used to having the odd joint as that was the in thing at the time. But But went off and got us some more weed and we had a more than pleasant afternoon on the beach, smoking weed and doing a bit of snorkelling and sunbathing.

We then headed back to the hotel at about six and on arrival, I went off with Liz to her room and Chris went with his girl to our room. We arranged to meet up in the bar about nine so we went our separate ways for a couple of hours. We went down to the bar and it was obvious that we were being talked about by everyone in the place. They were saying how they had seen us that day and how great we were. It was getting quite difficult to keep answering questions about the Harriers and how they can take off and land vertical. Of course Chris comes out with that one; we only fly them we don't make them, which everyone laughed at. We told everyone that we would have to go to bed at midnight as we had sorties to fly the next day. So I went off with Liz and Chris with Bee and they were probably at it again like we were until the early hours, shagging and talking. Liz asked how old I was. I told her twenty four as at twenty one; I thought I would be too young to be a pilot. I had to go along with it but I kept changing the subject. We talked a lot and she seemed quite keen. I liked her too but nothing could come of it for many reasons, the first one being all the shit she thought about us being pilots.

FLASHBACKS

I kept waiting for the Colonel shrink to tell me to get back to the point, but he was obviously enjoying my story about me and Chris.

The next morning Chris and I set off about seven as we had to be at the Blue Hole by ten. It was a bit awkward as I had to knock Chris up as he had also been up half the night. Bee jumped out of bed and ran along the corridor to jump in to bed with Liz. They were on the landing waving to us as we loaded up the Land Rover and set off to do our job. We were both laughing as we couldn't believe our luck.

I said to him, 'I nearly told her last night that we were not who we said we were.'

He said, 'You can't do that, Bee thinks we are the real thing.' I agreed to keep up the pretence for him, but I didn't like it.

We arrived at the Blue Hole and set up the radio equipment. We knew that there was always someone listening out at the base camp, as there was a fully manned communications centre there, where the RAF staff worked around the clock. It was also there for any emergencies as was the case in the past when a pilot had bailed out in the jungle. We did our standard radio check with them and we were then told to expect a patrol at around midday, as they had been delayed. That gave us a couple of hours to mess around so we decided to have a bit of a trek around the Blue Hole. The patrol arrived and the SAS trooper said that they would be doing another patrol that afternoon, but he believed they would be pulling back to airport camp the following day, which would be Thursday. We would have to do the sortie and then they would take us back

FLASHBACKS

to the Pelican Beach hotel. They would then take the Land Rover and we would be picked up the next day by helicopter from the hotel. This was going to be awkward, we thought as they may blow our cover. We did the sortie about four in the afternoon and two of the patrol came with us back to the Pelican Beach. We needn't have worried as the guys dropped us off and shot off to the village to get some weed probably.

We had to call up headquarters to confirm what was happening to Chris and I. It appeared from what the guys of the patrol had told us that the conflict as such was now over and we were just going to be kept in Belize as a presence. So it seemed Chris and I were getting grounded, just when we started to enjoy ourselves.. We decided to make the most of our last night, so after receiving all the accolades from the people staying in the hotel, we told them that we would be leaving the following day as the mission as such was being slowed down drastically. The girls were upset as we were getting to know them. Of course they didn't really know who we were, which in a way I was glad about. I was relieved to be leaving as I felt really guilty for pretending to be a pilot. I still felt like James Bond that night while we were having our brandy sours on the beach front, then me going off to bed with Liz, for the last time.

Once again I came back to reality and I found myself sat in front of the Colonel. I had obviously been waffling on about my career. The Colonel went on to say that it appeared that I had been having a good career in Belize and Malta. However he could not understand how the incidents I had described would lead me to a fear of flying. He said he could understand a little, why I may have had some anxiety at seeing the Vulcan

FLASHBACKS

explode in Malta, but not enough to the degree where I had refused to fly, as shown on my records. I told him the Vulcan incident was only part of the problem I had, but it wasn't the only reason, the fact that I had seen the Vulcan explode, bothered me, but it was on a return trip from Nairobi that caused the greatest problem in my mind. With that I think he had had enough of me for one day. He asked me to think about what had happened to me with regards to flying and that we could chat more when he saw me next time.

I went back to the ward and caught up with young John. He seemed in a bit of a state as he told me that the Colonel was considering sending him back to his unit.

I thought about it and told John I thought it was a good thing. He said he was tired and scared and didn't know if he could cope. I reassured him, but he was adamant he wasn't up to it. With that young John did a Rifleman T trick, instead of the table going through the window he started on another patient who had been getting on everyone's nerves. He was a gunner out of the Artillery who, through his own admission was working his ticket. The gunner had only been in the army two years and didn't like it, but he couldn't afford to buy himself out. He didn't want to put eighteen months' notice in to leave the army, so working his ticket, which was basically making out he was insane to get discharged, was in his mind, his only way out.

There were a couple of guys like him on the ward, but they didn't last long as patients, they would come and go and it was quite obvious to the shrinks or anyone with half a brain that they were wankers. I felt embarrassed to be in the same

FLASHBACKS

company as I certainly didn't want to be leaving the army, as it had been my life and saviour, or so I believed. The young artillery gunner had his party trick when we were all sitting in the TV lounge. He would sit himself up for a fart and then take out his lighter and put it to his arse when he farted. He was quite good at it and sometimes the flame would be a foot long from the methane coming out of his arse.

I am not sure why John chose him, maybe it's because he felt, like me, that the guy was not ill in any way just a wanker, who seemed to enjoy the fact that a lot of us soldiers were fucked in the head. I had been in the TV lounge with John the night previous and watched the gunner perform his party trick. Being the highest rank in there at the time, I told the gunner to pack it in. I said we had all seen his party trick and that he was becoming boring. I told him instead of putting the lighter to his arse to light up the methane, he should just hold the lighter in front of his mouth as there was more shit coming out of that end than the other.

He said, 'You can fuck off as well Corporal. I don't have to listen to you in here as you are a patient and you cannot boss me about.'

I said, 'You don't have to obey my orders if you don't want to' and just to make sure we understand each other, I head butted him. I said, 'Do you want to obey my orders now?'

He ran off to get the Duty Medic, who that night, was an RAF Corporal. He asked me what had happened and I told him I tripped over someone's foot and caught Gunner Smith on the nose as I fell. The soldiers who were in the room confirmed my side of the story, as most of them had had enough of Gunner

FLASHBACKS

Smith. I think John went out of his way to attack the gunner, I believe John chose him because of the incident in the TV lounge with me. I seriously think he did it for me as I had become his mentor and his hero, purely as I had rank and I told him stories about my army career. Or it could have simply been the case that John wanted to vent his anger out on someone. Whatever the reason was for attacking the gunner, it got him sectioned for want of a better word. He was put in isolation and I didn't get to see John for about four days. When he came out he was not the same person who had gone in. I knew he was angry as we all seemed to be full of rage; well the patients who had done a bit of soldiering anyway. The artillery wanker who was working his ticket only had anger for getting smacked.

John had returned from isolation he didn't have any anger; he didn't have anything, it was just as though they had cut out his tongue and his brain. I thought once again this is serious. I went to talk to young John and all he could say was he was tired.

'I am really tired,' he muttered. I asked him if they had given him anything, he just said that they had given him an injection on the day they put him in isolation. He said that's all they had done and he said instead of having two tablets a day he was now on three. He wasn't on the same drugs as me, he was on something called Largactol, which was obviously quite a strong drug as young John had become a zombie in a few days.

Seeing what had happened to John I felt such a rage come over me and I went over to the medical desk and kicked off, asking what the fuck they were doing to this young private.

FLASHBACKS

They told me to calm down and behave. I thought who the hell are you to tell me what to do and grabbed the RAF Corporal Medic by the shirt and picked him up out of his chair. I had just got him to his feet when I was grabbed on both sides and pinned down by a few of the other medics. That was my last memory before waking up in isolation.

I thought this is crazy, I am not crazy I am just angry, I knew why I was angry with regards to John but I also knew this inside rage was not right, as were the constant feelings of suicide that I had developed. I didn't want to tell anyone that I was having suicidal thoughts as I thought that would be the end of my career. I was in isolation for a couple of days. They told me I could come out if I promised to behave. I thought to myself at that time I have to go along with them otherwise my career will be done. I could remember snippets of what had happened to me to end up in the hospital, but the longer I was staying there the more I couldn't remember things, I thought it must be the drugs.

With yet another increase in medication, I knew that I had to get out of the hospital and I would do whatever it took to get out, In my mind, I was trapped, I didn't even know how many drugs I was on, I only knew I wanted to stop. I constantly requested that I didn't want to take any more tablets, only to be told, I could not just stop taking the drugs. I was told when the time was right I would have to be weaned off them gradually. I still had my faculties, so I decided that from then on I was going to wean myself off them, but I would have to play ball with the male nurse who dispensed the tablets out every day. I thought I would take them as normal which was in front of them and show my tongue to prove I had swallowed them. I did that for a few days and then I started to slip one under my tongue. As the Medic thought I was being a good soldier and just swallowing my medication he stopped checking after a few days. I had taken heed, about having to be weaned off them, so I thought I would drop down one tablet every ten days. I knew there was something not right about the medication or so I thought as after I had dropped down by one tablet, I became quite depressed or was I depressed anyway, I didn't know.

The side effect of the tablets was lethargy and it showed in my appearance. I had always been super fit, having done many courses that required a high level of fitness, from mountaineering to skiing. I was also a bit of an athlete, in that I had done the pole vault for the army against the RAF and had been junior pole vault champion, when I was a boy soldier. I could not believe what had happened to my body in a couple of months, having looked at my reflection, I was putting on weight and it showed. I needed to get out a lot more and take young John with me as my trainer. I decided I would have to suck shit with the staff and show them that I was being good. I would have to show them I was behaving, keep my head down for a while and adopt a low profile. Over that next couple of weeks, the gunner who John had battered was discharged out of the army, so I guess he had got what he wanted.

What I did find strange was, we were told Rifleman T had gone back to his unit. I thought it strange because although he had been behaving the last few weeks, I didn't think him well, as he still looked disturbed the last time I saw him. The other

FLASHBACKS

thing that aroused my suspicions was the fact that he had left some of his kit and one of the Medics had come and cleaned out his locker. I thought he must have been put in another hospital. Good luck to him I thought and forgot all about it.

My time for the shrink had come around and the Colonel wasn't too happy with me as he had heard about my kicking off in support of young John. He told me if I wanted to stay in the army he needed to have me concentrate on my own illness. Illness, I thought, I am not ill. Admittedly I didn't know what was wrong with me but when he said illness I thought, my God I am really in trouble.

He asked me to carry on about the fear of flying. He said he could understand, having seen the Vulcan explode that it may make me apprehensive, but he said it's not as though I was in the plane, I told him, I believed I knew when my fear started and when it peaked. I told him of the time I was inside a Belfast, which was a lot larger than a Hercules transport plane and when you saw them on the ground you wondered how they would take off. I had been sent to Cyprus, on a Belfast and I had managed to get a good seat. A good seat was somewhere in the middle of the plane as if you sat at the back you shit yourself as being an RAF plane it was not kitted out to look good on the inside, it was like the Hercules. You could see all the wires running through the plane and when the plane banked or did any movement you could watch all those wires and bars and things moving about like the cogs in a machine. The Loadmaster and Engineer on the planes always said it was for safety, as they could get to any problem straight away. At that time I could live with being a little apprehensive.

FLASHBACKS

I remembered becoming slightly more apprehensive whilst flying in the Belfast from the RAF base in Oxfordshire to Cyprus. We had been flying for just over four hours and we were on our approach to Cyprus. I was just trying to relax the best I could, suddenly there was an almighty bang and the inside of the plane went in to pitch darkness.

My initial thoughts were that something had hit us on the outside of the plane. I got it half right as the engineer appeared with a torch.

He told everyone not to panic, he said, we have just been struck by lightning.' It was only a matter of a few seconds, but it seemed like minutes that we were flying in darkness. Like a generator re-starting, the plane then came back to life and we carried on to land safely in Akrotiri.

I was talking to the Colonel about the Belfast being hit by lightning but in reality I was in my own world. I remembered

Belfast Aircraft

FLASHBACKS

the last time I had been been in RAF Akrotiri, with seven lads out of my troop. We were waiting for transport to take us to Dhekelia to join the rest of our unit. We all decided to go to the NAAFI on the base and have a few beers. Unfortunately the lads started to get drunk and upset some of the RAF guys. Before I knew it, a RAF Policeman had walked into the NAAFI, he came straight over and asked me what the hell those pomgoes thought they were doing. As his tone was aggressive, I told him straight, I believe it is called the Dambusters as by then the lads were running around shouting 'tally ho, tally ho'.

I then told him I was in charge and that I found his manner quite aggressive as the lads were just letting off steam, pretending to be crabs. (Army slang for the RAF in the same way they call soldiers pongees). He did not listen, instead he ordered me to get the lads out of the NAAFI or he would lock us up. I said something to him along the lines that we did not want to fall out and that there was no need for him to be insulting, by calling us pongos. He must have thought me reasonable until I challenged him to a fight, something I would regret later.

I told the policeman, the behaviour of the lads in Cyprus was nothing new as we would behave the same in England. As far as they were concerned, it was fair game to take the piss out of the crabs. The same way the crabs took the piss out of us by calling us pongos. He said it was not acceptable behaviour on an RAF base and that he would be reporting me. I suppose he had a point, I did point out that although we were pongos, we were actually stationed on an RAF base in England. His only response to that was to say thank you for letting him know

FLASHBACKS

where he had to report me too, he then escorted us to a transit room.

Once again I was brought back in to the real world by the voice of my shrink, the Colonel. He was saying something about the Belfast and it was as though I was having two conversations, one with him and the other with my memories. My memories were winning as I started to think about happier times at the RAF base in Oxfordshire.

It was called RAF Benson and it was also home to the Queen's Flight. Whenever the Queen went anywhere they would send a plane or a helicopter from Benson to London to pick her up. In reality there were more politicians and other members of the royal family that used the service more than Her Majesty. They also used the planes to ferry guests of the royal family around. Which was a pain in the ass for us soldiers stationed at RAF Benson. As was often the case, we would have to become a guard of honour for the frequent visitors to the Queen. A regular visitor at that time was King Hussein of Jordan. He did seem quite a nice bloke, although he was only about five feet tall.

The reason I mentioned the Queen's Flight is because they had two Andover planes on the Queen's flight. They were kept on the base and were often parked just outside our hanger. I remember one of the aircraft being parked outside hanger, that same day we had a new second in command arrive at Benson. He had joined our unit straight out of officer training and as such he believed himself to have instantly become a leader of men.. Of course he would be, but he was too far up his own arse and believed we should give him respect straight

FLASHBACKS

away, purely because he was an officer. Well we all know that respect is earned, not given freely, especially in the army. The officer had only been there a few hours or so when the Sergeant Major decided he had to teach the officer a lesson, as he had apparently been getting on his nerves. The Sergeant Major turned told me to go and get the paperwork for the aircraft. I knew what he meant as we did the same thing with nearly everyone who joined the squadron. A 1033 is the army form you have to sign, whenever you are given anything, be it uniform, weapons, vehicles, whatever it is, if it was issued, you have to sign for it. The form would contain every part of the thing you are issued. The completed 1033 form we had was made up for the Andover aircraft, parked outside our hanger. The paperwork went through everything on the plane, starting off with the basics, like propellers x 2, landing wheels x 8, wings x 2 and so on until you got down to wheel nuts complete with washers x 64 and even things that you could describe but could not show as they were behind the auxiliary landing gear approach hydraulic pump. Of course none of it was real, they were just things made up by the lads in the office.

The Sgt Major said, 'Off you go Sir' to the Lieutenant, 'follow the Corporal and he will take you through your aircraft.'

He explained that the RAF Andover was under our protection and that's why it was positioned outside our hangar. As the guy he had replaced had relinquished the position of signing for the aircraft, it was now his job to sign for it. He told the officer that the boss, Captain Jack had left him instructions to get the Lieutenant to sign for the aircraft. So off I went with the Officer and spent an hour walking around pointing at the more obvious parts that could be explained. So every time we got to the bottom of the page, I would get the Lieutenant to sign the 10.33 and he was starting to get a bit fed up and asked me how much longer. With that another Corporal, in on the act came out and told me he would take over the handover of the aircraft. It was about two and a half hours later, when the Officer completed signing for his aircraft. He walked back into the troop office at the same time as Captain Jack returned from a briefing.

The Lieutenant, feeling full of beans, having spent hours outside signing for his aircraft, went up to Captain Jack and said, 'I have signed for my plane Sir.'

Captain Jack was a ranker, meaning that he had come up through the ranks to become an Officer and as such he was one of the lads. He burst out laughing and said, 'Are you fucking real?' to the Officer as we were all laughing. He eventually saw the funny side and it did knock the edge off him a bit and he became a little less up his own arse and realised he was not as important as he thought he was.

Once again the Colonel interrupted me and asked if I had problems with officers, I said no, I told him I did have problems respecting them if they were no good, but I would never show it. He then asked if what had happened with the Belfast was the reason for not wishing to fly and he also asked if I was charged for the incident with the RAF police.

I told him that the aircraft being struck by lightning didn't help, but it was not the main reason. I then went on to tell him what happened with regards to the incident in Cyprus.

Nothing happened to the rest of the the lads, but I was

charged the next day and had to appear in front of the Commanding Officer. Typical of the army, they always charge you under section sixty nine, contrary to good order and military discipline. I was marched in front of the boss by the RSM and he read out the charge. Basically stating I was in charge of a section of men and that we had got pissed in the NAAFI at RAF Akrotiri. When asked to leave, I apparently threatened a superior rank with violence.

In such cases you can get demoted or put in jail for a week or so or whatever the Commanding Officer decides. Also when you are charged in the army you don't really have any legal representation, you are allowed a character witness to speak up for you, which sometimes softens the punishment. My character witness that day was Bert the Regimental Sergeant Major who had marched me in front of the CO. I was taken quite shocked at the time as I didn't even think he cared that much about me. Although he had been with the squadron for six months, he had come from an airborne background, working with the Special Forces and the airborne. I was one of the first men he met in the squadron as we got pissed together when he first arrived. I remember the first day I met him as he arrived incognito and just walked into the Corporal's Mess. I thought him a little old to still be a corporal but thought nothing else about it as we had a drink and he told me what unit he had come from. He told me how long he had been in the army and I remember asking him what he had done wrong to still be a corporal after sixteen years. That was when he told me he was the new sergeant major and he thought he would like to meet the lads. At the time I thought that he must be a decent bloke as instead of going to the Sergeant's Mess he decided to check us guys out in our mess.

I went in front of the CO and he found me guilty as I admitted that we were drunk and a little high spirited. The CO then asked the RSM who my character witness was. I was wondering who it could be as I had not even had time to speak to anyone to give me a character reference. The RSM stated that he was my character witness, I nearly fainted. I am stood to attention in front of the boss listening to the RSM who I did have a lot of respect for. He went on to say that I was a total fucking idiot at times. He said that I play hard all the time, another reason to get in to trouble. Then he came out with a pearl, he said how much of an idiot I was but if it came to the crunch and we had to go in to action, I would be one of the few men in the squadron that he would want with him. He said I was an idiot but he had no qualms about my soldiering ability.

After hearing how much the RSM thought about me, I wasn't really thinking about what the CO was going to do to me for punishment, as I was proud that a man I respected had shown me some respect in return, as he obviously saw past me being an idiot. With that the CO thanked the RSM and then went on to say, because of our situation at the time in Cyprus, he would deal with the charge on our return to England as he needed me in my role at that present time. The bigger issues being that the Turkish Armed Forces had just taken over half the island. Being half Greek myself I naively believed we were going to do something about that, Cyprus having been a British colony for a couple of hundred years. I remember at that time being embarrassed to be a British soldier as our only job in

FLASHBACKS

Cyprus was to assist the fleeing Greek Cypriots, who were being evicted from their homes. I never really got over that trip, but I did learn that being a soldier doesn't make a difference as that was when I realised we were just pawns on a chess board, to be used and abused where ever the politicians thought fit.

After the tour, I returned to England to face the music. I was duly put in front of the Commanding Officer and was charged with the incident in Akrotiri. My punishment was that prior to going to Cyprus I was a Lance Corporal. The CO told me prior to the incident in Cyprus I was to have been promoted on my return. I was to be promoted to full Corporal, which was just as well as the CO told me due to my character reference being so good from the RSM he had saved me from being demoted to Signalman. He told me I would not be promoted for at least six months from that time and I would be fined two hundred pounds, a week's pay.

The doctor then piped up and asked me if I was upset about the charge and the fact that I was not promoted on my return from Cyprus. I just told him being half Greek, I was more upset for the Greek people on Cyprus who in my opinion had been let down badly by the British government, He then said something about injustice and asked me to say what happened next with my career.

I explained as part of my punishment for bad discipline in Cyprus, the CO told me I would be volunteering to go to Kenya for six months with the Engineers from Waterbeach. Our troop needed to supply a communications cell, to provide a morse link back to the UK and a voice link in Kenya. Our group was to also provide communications for the Army Air Corps, who

FLASHBACKS

were sending out a Sioux helicopter. The Engineers would also need communications provided as and when required. There was already an established communications centre in Mombasa and we would supply a link from the Mara River, which was to be our base. I was to be second in command as there would be eight of us altogether; my mate Derek, a full Corporal at the time, later to become Sergeant before we left for Kenya, me and six signalmen. The idea was that we were going out there in November with the advance party of engineers who would be setting up the camp at the Mara River in anticipation of the main regiment coming out after Christmas.

Once again I knew I was still talking to the Colonel in hospital, talking whilst daydreaming, I told him how Kenya became quite a critical part of my army career as it could be part of the reason I had ended up in hospital in London. The idea of going to Africa appealed to me as I had been lots of places although I was still only twenty two. I'd been married since I was nineteen, my marriage would finish when I went to Kenya. It wasn't a great love affair, it was more two people who hadn't had good lives coming together and my wife became pregnant. It wasn't really a marriage in my mind as I had only married, because she was pregnant. In the three years of marriage I perhaps only spent six months at home, I was either in Northern Ireland or playing soldiers somewhere in the world. I told her that I would be going off to Kenya for six months and she told me that she would not be waiting around for me anymore as I loved the army more than I loved her. Sheila liked being an army wife in Germany and when I left her to come to England to try for the airborne and then subsequently get posted to England, the marriage failed. She was a good person, the main problem was we were too young and had she not got pregnant, I don't believe we would have seen each other after our fling in Germany. That was probably the main reason I volunteered to go anywhere as I preferred to be away as in my mind, I wasn't old enough to be married. I certainly couldn't hack nagging, so I went off to Kenya a single man, in my mind anyway.

In fact there was only Derek who was married. Being married or not never really came into it in the army; as soldiers, we would go around the world and behave like single men looking for their next shag. I had met my wife in Germany as she came to visit her sister who was married to a serviceman. The guy's first name was Willie B and he was a total weirdo, I didn't realise how weird until I went to his army house one day, to meet my wife to be. He was there in the house with his wife and their two kids and they were all in the nude, 'What a fucking weirdo,' I thought.

Those thoughts aside it was to be the place I ended up getting my wife to be pregnant. Having only known her for about six weeks, she returned to where she came from, that being Aberdeen. A week or so after she went home, I received the letter, telling me she was pregnant. As soldiers we used to call them CHIP letters, Come Home I Pregnant. Of course the bad answer to a CHIP letter is a FISH letter, Fuckoff I Staying Here. At the time, I was pretty naïve and said I would do the right thing, marry her. The whole thing was done and dusted in around four months of meeting. I flew to Aberdeen on leave and as I only had seven days leave, it was all a bit rushed.

FLASHBACKS

My best mate Ray in the army couldn't get any leave. My wife to be was obviously keen to get married as she even arranged for her mate's boyfriend to be the best man. I didn't bother telling any of my family at the time that I was getting married as they would not have come anyway. My twin was in the nut house, my sister still at school and the eldest had already left home.

On reflection I was stupid to go through with it. I knew I didn't love the woman and she being younger than me was probably feeling the same, but she was pregnant and in those days you had to get married, or so you were brainwashed to think. It was a fiasco from the start. I had around two hundred pounds to pay for the wedding and the idea was, we would get married and after we would just go for a meal with the best man and his girlfriend, who were rough as shit. I never proved it but after we had the meal and went back to their flat my wallet disappeared with all my cash. It turned up outside their flat door with all the cash gone and as I knew it was in the inside pocket of my blazer when I went into the flat, the only person who could have nicked it was the best man. At least I got my ID card back and my wallet as that also had my air ticket inside. I guess I could have made more of an effort with the marriage but I couldn't deal with the woman. I would come back from wherever I had been and she would be nice to me for a day before she started the nagging about being on her own. It was mainly my fault with the marriage not succeeding as I was on my own most of the time. It was the same for a lot of guys in the army, you may be married, but when you got away from home, you became single.

FLASHBACKS

The shrink asked me if my marriage breakdown had upset me and made me depressed. I told him, it didn't bother me that much, although I missed my daughter as I didn't want her to grow up the same as me, without a father.

I carried on speaking, I went on to tell him, I had three weeks embarkation leave prior to going to Kenya and by the time that was up, so was my marriage. Whenever you were going anywhere in the army for several months, be it Northern Ireland or anywhere, you always got embarkation leave and perhaps a month off when you got back from a tour. I think we both knew it was the end as I said goodbye to her and my two year old daughter.

On completion of my embarkation leave, Derek, me and the lads went off to Cambridge, which was where the Engineers were based. We had to prepare our own equipment for the trip. To that end we had a couple of weeks at Waterbeach Barracks with the sappers. They seemed a good bunch of lads and they showed us a lot of respect as was the case most of the time, being attached to other regiments. They gave you a lot of respect and breathing space, to do your own job.

It was after we got to Cambridge that we found out the whole extent of what the Engineers would be doing and indeed what we would be doing whilst in Kenya. The tour was going to be seven months for us and as we were part of the advance party, we would be leaving in two weeks. The main regiment would be following us after Christmas and as it was the beginning of November it would mean we would be two months setting up the camp by the Mara River in Northern Kenya. Most of the brief we knew, our job would be to supply

FLASHBACKS

communications whilst in Kenya with a link back to Cyprus. To do the job, we would be taking two Land Rovers, kitted out with the radio equipment and we would also be taking Clansman mobile radio equipment. We were also briefed that there would be another Engineer unit out in Kenya that may need our assistance, for communications. Their main purpose for being in Kenya was to make maps and at the same time they also intended to climb Kilimanjaro whilst out there.

We spent the next ten days in Cambridge getting everything prepared to leave. There was always a lot to do prior to such tours; injections, lectures and just getting the vehicles ready to be transported by Hercules was a nightmare as you had to secure them for flight. The lectures were mainly about the jungle, but being squaddies we also had to have lots of lectures about the Nairobi nightlife. As Nairobi would be our first port

The Mara River

FLASHBACKS

of call prior to setting off up country, we were shown many films of the local people. We had films about the Mara River and where we would be camped for several months. We were advised to lay off having sex with the locals as we were informed that lots of the women had syphilis and as well as being highly contagious, there was no cure. The other thing we had to be careful not to catch was Malaria. To that end we had already been taking a drug for two weeks prior to departure. Of course we listened and went through the motions of being responsible when we watched the films but the truth is that everything we had leaned whilst in England would disappear as and when we were set loose, wherever the army sent us.

Apart from the danger of death from syphilis, the only other thing that might be the death of us out there was of course the animals. As we would be camped at the side of the river, the main animal we had to worry about were the hippos, they lived a few hundred yards from where we were building our camp. There were also many snakes we had to look out for, the main ones being a black mamba and apparently there were many puff adders. Up to that point I thought a black mamba was a dance and a puff adder was a gay snake.

The Masai tribe had a village across the river from where we were pitching our camp. They were the reason we were going to that part of Kenya, as the Engineers would be building a bridge across the Mara River to enable the Masai to get across safely. Not only did they have to dodge hippos but apparently there was some sort of beast that lived in the bottom of the river and once stood on would bite into your feet. I believe it was called schistosomiasis or something like that. If you stood

FLASHBACKS

on it and got infected your foot would end up looking like an elephants foot and would continue to grow like a massive wart. I had seen pictures before of the condition but when they showed us some pictures of the locals who had caught the disease, it made me more concerned, I thought I would rather get bitten by a snake as I had already survived that.

Then having had my scares already with flying I wasn't keen on the fact that we would be eighteen hours in a Hercules, getting to Kenya. But I put my fears to the back of my mind, which was my way of dealing with those things. I was getting quite excited about the trip. Having not been back from Ireland very long and having suffered there, I thought I deserved a safari. The day finally came when we, the advance party would be setting off, we were about fifty altogether; eight Signallers, six Army Catering Corps, two Army Air Corp, four Mechanics and around thirty Engineers. We would all be flying out in one Hercules and there would be three Land Rovers on the plane, two of which were ours and the other belonged to the engineers.

The idea was that we would all be barracked in a place called Kahawa which was a base just outside Nairobi, where all military personnel in Kenya would always stay on their arrival. It was quite a big camp. Not only were soldiers based there, it was where all the equipment was kept. As it was not cost effective to keep flying equipment out to places like Kenya, the military always shipped out equipment from England that had served its purpose in England. Where the equipment was serviceable although old, it would be shipped abroad to bases in places like Kenya, Canada or the Far East where it would once again be used until it no longer was serviceable. Then the

FLASHBACKS

equipment, be it a bulldozer or a lorry, would be left to rot or used for spare parts in that particular country. As a lot of the equipment used abroad was old, some of the vehicles looked like they had been there since World War Two.

The journey out to Kenya was a drag in that we would be getting there via Cyprus, where the RAF would have to drop some equipment off. I had been talking to the loadmaster on the Hercules about my incidents whilst flying with the RAF and he kindly arranged for me to climb up the stairs into the cockpit of the Hercules and sit at the back of the cockpit whilst carrying on our journey to Nairobi. It was all very casual; not at all as you would imagine it to be. I got talking to the pilots who were only about twenty eight years old themselves and very laid back. I explained about why I had become slightly afraid of flying and the only reason I wanted to do the airborne course was to get a parachute when I had to fly, so I could at least jump out of a plane if I needed too. They both laughed and said they would rather just stay with the plane.

We were talking and both of the pilots had joined the RAF to become pilots and it was both their intentions to become airline pilots with British Airways or another company. I asked them if they would like to fly Concorde as that would have to be every pilots dream. I brought that up as it was only the year before that I had flown on Concorde as at that time my troop were based at RAF Brize Norton and Concorde was there to do its pre service training, before going into service with British Airways. I was lucky enough to win the raffle which was held quite regular which gave the winner a jolly on Concorde as it did its take-off and landing practice at Brize Norton. Of course

FLASHBACKS

I told them it was okay but it seemed very cramped.

Then I realised how cramped I was on the Hercules, down in the main part of the plane. I had about two feet between me and the Land Rover that was directly in front of my face. I could lift my legs up and rest them on the side of the vehicle. The vehicles were chained to the floor of the Hercules and every time it banked you could feel the tension on the chains. The seats down the Hercules were just netting that ran all the way down the sides of the aircraft, so effectively you were flying sideways. There were half a dozen or so port hole windows, but they were way above the seats, so you couldn't look out of a window and see anything, well you could see the sky. It was always a race when you were on a long flight with a Hercules. The fastest out of their seats after take-off could climb on to the top of the Land Rovers. As the vehicles were soft skinned they had a canvas roof so you could settle in between the steel frame, it was like being in a hammock. You could also see out of the porthole windows from the tops of the vehicles. It was also quite cooler the higher you could get in the plane. I was fortunate on that journey as I was able to spend about four hours in the cockpit. I was amazed at the view from the front of the aircraft, watching the propellers and basically wandering how such a heavy plane could fly. I was also lucky when I climbed back down out of the cockpit into the hold of the plane. I noticed a space on the top of one of the Land Rovers and quickly shot over to it, got my sleeping bag out and went off to sleep. It was not really allowed but if you had a good Loadmaster on the plane, they tended to ignore that rule. My flight to Kenya was memorable for the right reasons, I enjoyed sitting in the cockpit and then getting my head down for the rest of the journey.

We arrived in Nairobi and quickly unloaded our Land Rovers and were given a map and the location of Kahawa Barracks. The rest of the guys on the plane were ferried to a couple of waiting trucks. Once we set off, I was glad I wasn't in the back of the lorries sat on the wooden seats as the roads around Nairobi were okay, but as soon as we got out of the city they became like training tracks for tanks. You could see the guys in the backs of the trucks bouncing up and down. That aside I was really excited, I was twenty two and there I was in Africa. I thought I was Humphrey Bogart in the *African Queen*. Being a bit of a comic I always did impressions and one of my impressions was Humphrey.

We were driving along, I saw someone who looked like a working lady, I opened the window and gave the girl my Humphrey Bogart quote.

'Of all the gin joints, in the world, you had to walk into mine, play it again Sam. 'Derek was quick to point out that was from Casablanca not the *African Queen*.

We arrived at Kahawa after about half an hour, having driven past a massive town built of corrugated sheets, cardboard and wooden pallets. It was known as shit city to the poor people who had built it and made it their home. I thought I had been poor as a child, but these people were living in a shed they had built to survive, a dog in England would live in better conditions. It made me feel quite sad and realise although my childhood had been a trauma, I had been fed and provided with a roof over my head. Most of the roofs over these people's heads were made of scrap and covered with anything that would keep the rain out.

The main reason we had gone to Kenya at that time, was because we had to build the bridge over the Mara River before the rainy season started. I wondered how the people I had seen were going to survive when the rains came.

On arrival in Kahawa, my first impressions were not that good, the accommodation was quite basic. It was a long hangar type building and along the floor every few feet or so was an army issue camp bed. The beds consisted of four steel legs and were about seven inches off the ground. Sadly not only were the beds to be used in Kahawa, we were taking them with us when we left to go up country. Each bed had a mosquito net hanging from a frame that ran the length of the building and supported the mosquito nets. Still, I wasn't too bothered as I was in Africa and getting ready for our one hundred and fifty mile trip to the Masai Mara river, as it was known. Before that was going to happen we had at least seven days to enjoy the nightlife of Nairobi, while we awaited all the other equipment that was being ferried out by the transport planes.

The main man in charge of us at that time was a Sergeant Major from the Royal Engineers. He just told us we could do our own thing whilst we were in Kahawa as they would be preparing all the vehicles and equipment for the trip to the Mara River. There were bulldozers, dumper trucks and graders, it was like being with Wimpey, the only difference being we were in uniform and the equipment was old.

Derek and I decided with our lads that we would make the most of the Nairobi night life whilst we had the chance, as

FLASHBACKS

in a week or so we might not be seeing civilisation for a while. Nairobi was quite an eye opener as we headed for the centre of Nairobi, where the best hotels were situated. It wasn't exactly like I had imagined, I had imagined Kensington High Street. It turned out more like Notting Hill Market. Being squaddies we didn't need much in the way of glamour, as long as we had drink and women; that's all we really needed. We quickly found out that the local beer was called Tusker and the great thing about Kenyan beer was that it cost the same price if you drank it in a posh hotel or a dive. So you could sit in the best two hotels in Nairobi, the Hilton, the New Stanley and pay three Kenyan shillings for a beer.

I thought that was a brilliant idea as you couldn't get ripped off like you do in say the Ritz or Savoy in London. I had been in both the year before so I did know what it was like to be ripped off. We went firstly into the Hilton to have a few beers as we thought we may as well enjoy the luxury of the Hilton. It was like a perfume house in the middle of a sewer. We managed to last in the Hilton for about two hours, before being asked to leave. A couple of the guys had decided they liked sliding down the long curved bannister rail that ran up the stairs to the bar we were sat in. We then decided to get something to eat and ended up in a place called the Pink Lobster. The bar come restaurant was directly across the road from the New Stanley Hotel. I told my mate the hotel was named after the famous explorer, the thick twat said 'Christopher Columbus'.

We were sat on the balcony watching the Kenyan nightlife, which was a mad rush, very old yellow taxis everywhere.

FLASHBACKS

It seemed like everything in Kenya was on its last legs. Talking of which I was just watching the hustle and bustle on the road, when I noticed a commotion just across the road. It was a guy who was about three feet tall in front of a taxi, the guy was banging his arms and hands on the bonnet of the taxi and was refusing to move as the taxi driver was beating his horn and shouting for him to shift. With that the taxi driver got out his taxi and grabbed the little guy who was bashing on his bonnet. He grabbed him under his arms and dragged him to the kerb. That was when I noticed the poor guy didn't have any legs. He got about on a stump and his outstretched arms. The poor guy had got upset with the taxi driver as he was trying to get across the busy road on his arms and bum when the taxi driver started blasting his horn. The little guy took offence and decided to stop in the middle of the road, in front of the taxi and demonstrate his annoyance at the driver.

I thought, 'Good for you little man.' I couldn't believe the taxi driver wouldn't have any sympathy for the poor bloke with no legs. No sooner had the taxi driver thrown the little guy on to the kerb and was walking back to get in his taxi, the little guy as quick as you like ran on his arms and bum, shot back in front of the taxi and continued his bashing on the bonnet.

I was laughing at him because he had such pluck for a guy without legs. I believe he just thought fuck you to the taxi driver for being so unsympathetic. With that the taxi driver came around again and started dragging the poor little guy to the kerb but this time a lot more aggressively, I took offence at his treatment, jumped over the balcony and pushed the taxi driver off the little guy. I gave the little guy a few Kenya shillings

FLASHBACKS

– about five as I remember – which was about fifty pence to me, but was a fortune to him. I was feeling quite pleased about my actions and believed I had done a good deed. An hour or so later, we were still in the same bar and just about to leave when I saw the same little guy talking to the taxi driver. The owner of the bar told us the cripple and the taxi driver made a fortune outside the New Stanley and the Hilton. The cripple and the taxi driver are family and it is how the cripple looks after himself; they do it a few times a week, either outside hotels or anywhere where they see some whites. Needless to say I wasn't going to be taken in again, not by those guys any way.

We moved on after we had eaten, we ended up in one of the seediest night clubs in Nairobi. It was called *The Flamingo* and had a massive plastic flamingo at the entrance. Inside was a load of other birds and they were all interested in us. As the night went on we had our choice of all the gorgeous black Kenyan women. When it came to leave the club my mate Chalkie and I decided we should take the risk and go off with two local women. Being the careful sorts we did adhere to the films we had seen about the local women in the film we had seen in England. In that film they depicted most of the women as having syphilis and all sorts of diseases, we were told to be really, especially careful with the Masai women, you could recognise them with the distinctive partings in their hair. I remember that film because I asked the question after the film. I remember asking the instructor, how you would know if a Masai woman had a disease. He told us about the hair and he said if you get past the hair, you put your finger up her bottom and your thumb in her vagina and if you can click them she is rotten.

On a more serious note Chalkie and I decided to accompany the two girls back to their place, their place being what you would call a garage in England. They did actually live in a garage. By the time we got there, we weren't bothered about where they lived, we just wanted sex. We believed we would be okay as the girls didn't have all those partings in their hair like the Masai. They had hair like Michael Jackson at the time – sort of big and Afro looking. All was going well with my woman, she had just taken all her clothes off and I was thinking what a nice body she had, when she put her hands up to her head and played with what were obviously hair grips. She then removed her wig to reveal she was a Masai.

I said to Chalkie, 'Come on mate I ain't risking syphilis.' We rapidly got dressed and ran off to try and find a taxi back to Kahawa. Of course being gentlemen we both gave the girls about two pounds each and they were over the moon as we made our excuses about having to get back to Kahawa.

The next day we carried on preparing the equipment for our journey to the Mara River. Having had a few more nights in Nairobi, we were ready to set off for the Masai Mara. We were to head for the nearest place to where we were going and wait the rest of the transport. The Engineers were behind us in their low loaders, transporting the heavy plant. We had two Land Rovers and the place we were all heading for was called Narok. It wasn't so much a place, rather than a supermarket in the shape of a portakabin in the middle of nowhere. It was the main trading place for the locals and the equivalent of Watford

FLASHBACKS

Gap services to the Kenyans. It was also about five hours away from Nairobi and although we could have got there quite quickly we decided to take our time as the low loaders would take at least eight hours on the non-existent Kenyan roads, more like cattle tracks. It was still good as it was as though we were on a massive safari paid for by the army.

The first animals we came across when we got near to Narok, was a pride of lions. They were all dozing at the side of the track under a tree, so being squaddies we had to stop along the side of them. We sat in the vehicle for a while just watching them doing nothing except sleeping and looking up at us. I decided to take a closer look and got out of the vehicle. I was about twenty feet away when the big female got up with a roar and I shit myself running back to the vehicle as my mate had decided to start it up.

We had only gone about another mile or so when I came across my first Masai tribesmen walking along the road. There were two of them dressed in their scarlet cloaks and carrying spears as they walked along without an interest in the world. I was just thinking to myself, I wonder if we are the first white men they have seen close up. When I got level with them I stopped and became deflated about my day dream of being the first white men they had seen. They both had all this Masai regalia on but they both also had green army batteries hanging from their ears. They both had their ears split and through the hole they had attached SP11 batteries. They had scraped all the insides out of the batteries and then cut the tin outer case, to look like ear rings. They also had copper wire tied around their arms, the same wire we used to make antennas. They were

FLASHBACKS

very friendly and as I had learned to say hello in Swahili, I just said hello, *Jambo*. One pointed at the cigarette I was smoking, so I gave them both a cigarette. The guy nearly finished the cigarette in one drag and I watched as he turned nearly white as he went dizzy. He had not had one for a while I guessed or maybe he thought the dizziness was the aim of smoking, we didn't hang about to find out.

Our next bit of fun was when we decided to go off the track, as we had seen a black and white Land Rover in the distance. It obviously belonged to some safari company as it looked like it contained tourists. They were chasing the wilderbeast, the staple diet of nearly all the wild animals in Africa, or so it seemed. The wilderbeast in their tens of thousands work their way through the Masai Mara up to Tanzania every year and as such there were thousands of them. We had watched one being taken by a cheetah and we decided to drive in amongst the lot. We spent about an hour playing then decided we had better get off to the rendezvous in Narok. There had been some engineers in Kenya the year before and they had cut a road from Narok to the Mara River. So the last part of the journey to the Masai village would only take around fifteen minutes.

The project had been a two year project, the previous year they had built the road. We could see the road we had to take as there was only one road and the locals were walking up and down it. It was about ten miles to the river and these people had to walk it every other day if they wanted to trade. I suppose it's a way of life for them. We decided we had better wait for the Engineers as it was getting to the middle of the afternoon.

FLASHBACKS

Their convoy arrived and we set off with the Land Rovers to get to the river and start making a temporary camp for the night. The low loaders were still miles away so we would have to build a few tents for those guys as well. We had got there with a few hours of daylight left, so we got to work building the main requirements for that night. The first thing we had to do was dig a big hole for the toilet.

It was like being on a movie set for Tarzan or so I thought, there was a bridge across the river and it was your typical movie set bridge made from ropes and stretched between the trees on each side of the river. I had never seen a hippo close up and was amazed at the size of them.

By building a bridge for the local Masai, it would save the villagers having to walk many miles to cross the river. They could get across on the Tarzan bridge with its dodgy wooden floor, but they couldn't get across it carrying anything as you needed both hands to hold on to the bridge.

We had with us a local Masai man who had been employed by the British army to be a guide and liaison officer with the locals. The guy went over to the village and after some negotiation hired several of the village men to be our camp security at night. Their job would be to patrol all night and to keep wild animals away from us soldiers. After some team effort we managed to put up enough tents for us all to have one each, to save them getting nicked by the locals. If they could nick our batteries and antenna wire, they would surely take the tents. It was about midnight when we finally got our heads down. It did seem a bit spooky as you could hear the hippos, I don't know if they were yawning or just talking but

FLASHBACKS

they made a racket. Getting your head down in the bush was no different to the jungles of central America, except here we had camp beds and there we slept on the floor. We still had mosquito nets which was just as well as there were millions of the twats. I always made sure my net circumnavigated me, especially after seeing one of the guys in Kahawa barracks back in Nairobi. Like all of us in Nairobi he had been on the piss down town and when he got back, he was so drunk he couldn't be bothered to put up his mosquito net. The next day his back didn't have a space from all the bites he had taken during the night. He was oblivious to the fact that he was getting bit as he was so drunk, he didn't wake up.

So although I was alone and it wasn't as spooky as being alone in the Central American jungle, it was a little eerie next to the river. After what seemed ages I managed to fall asleep, but woke up in the night with a noise coming from something near me. It was dark so I could not see whatever was near me; I just knew there was something in my tent. I had a torch in my webbing equipment along with a machete, so I grabbed them both. As normal we all also had our personal weapons, which at that moment was surplus to requirement as we had no ammunition. So whilst I could hear whatever it was in my tent, the only thing I could defend myself with, would be the machete. I jumped off the bed and out of the mosquito net, at the same time jumping back and putting on the torch with my left hand, my right hand holding the machete. I absolutely crapped myself when I saw a six foot snake in the corner of my tent. I say tent, it was more of a marquee than a tent, so there was plenty of room. I put the machete in my left hand with the

FLASHBACKS

torch and grabbed a six foot tent pole and starting flicking the snake towards the entrance. Every time it turned its head back in my direction, I would pick it up with the pole and flick it towards the door. Up to that point I hadn't thought about killing it, I just wanted to get it out of my tent. I managed to flick it outside the tent, where I could get a better look at it under the newly fitted lights around the camp. As I flicked it out of the tent entrance, one of the local Masai who was on his way to investigate my torch light was about four feet away from the tent entrance and when he saw the snake I had just flicked out, he shouted, 'MaBoowoo,' or something like that and the snake went for him. I realised it wasn't a nice snake and chopped it in half with the machete. The local Masai said something like 'santa sana' which I think means thank you.

The next day I was told by the interpreter the snake I had killed was a puff adder and that they are deadly. Apparently they had accounted for several Masai deaths, due to them being so venomous. He told me you don't have long to live without treatment if you are bit by a puff adder

Needless to say I was the talk of the camp the next day. I didn't help myself as I had a bit of a reputation for being barking mad. I got some of the copper wire, we used for making our antennas. I tied some around the longer part of the snake that I had killed, I put it around its neck and I had about twenty feet of slack wire that I attached to the buckle, at the back of my webbing. As such the snake was dragged along behind me and it seemed to give everyone a laugh. I was confronted by the Sergeant Major of the Engineers, who was the boss at the time as he was the senior rank up the bush so

FLASHBACKS

to speak. Of course there wouldn't be any officers until we had built them a nice little tent. The Sergeant Major was a good guy and you could have a laugh with him, which we did in Nairobi town.

He asked me if I was for real and he wanted to know why I was towing a dead snake around on my webbing. I just pointed at the sky to a flock of circling vultures, he just laughed.

After about a week of doing nothing but building the camp, I was fed up putting up tents, after all we had built our communication base in a couple of hours. We were all meant to dig in to get the camp built, but my thoughts of having a laugh, were not putting tents up all day. I went over to the Sergeant Major and explained to him that I had never driven a dumper before and asked him if I could drive the dumper instead.

He smiled at me and said, 'That's fine, I have just the job for you.' We jumped in our spare Land Rover and he took me about a mile from where we were camped and showed me a big hole in the middle of nowhere. We drove back to the camp and he said, 'Do you remember where that hole is?'

I said, 'Yes Sir.'

He said, 'Get the dumper,' I thought this is going to be fun. He said, 'Get the dumper and go around all the latrines,' or thunder boxes for a better name. They were the wooden boxes with a hole in the middle; we would sit on them to crap. The crap and pee would fall in the strategically placed bucket and as such they would be quite full after a week of wee and crap. My job he told me was to go around all the thunder boxes and empty all the buckets in to the dumper truck, I would then

FLASHBACKS

have to transport the dumper full of shit and piss to the hole he had just showed me. He said as he liked me so much and as I liked to drive the dumper so much, I could drive it every week for the months we were going to be up country.

I did as I was told by the Sergeant Major, I went around all the thunder boxes and emptied all the contents into the dumper. Apart from the stink I thought it wouldn't be too bad as it seemed okay on the way to the hole with the wind behind me. What I hadn't accounted for was the bumpy track going to the hole as I had not noticed it too much in the Land Rover. I had plenty of time to think about it after that first time when I went faster than a crawl, it seemed the contents of the dumper just wanted to shoot in the air and let me catch it on my face and body. I laughed to myself as I thought the Sergeant Major was taking the piss, then I realised it was me taking the piss and the shit. At least it got me out of camp and tent building that day. I was not driving faster than five miles an hour to the hole as I thought the noise of the dumper would frighten any animals and I wasn't in any rush.

We carried on building the camp for the next few weeks. In that time we had become pretty friendly with our local guests from the Masai village. We could watch the women all day with their tits out and chat to the guys who patrolled the camp. It was getting near Christmas and a guy from one of the safari companies paid us a visit. He asked us if we could send a few messages for him as he would not be getting back to Nairobi for a while. We did what he asked and he decided to stay and have a drink with us, he also bought everyone a drink. He told us about the safari company he worked for and how he also knew Virginia Mckenna. Before he left, he told us he would be back and promised to bring us some fresh meat for Christmas. Sure to his word on Christmas Day he turned up in his open topped Land Rover, along with two gazelles he had shot. He told us it was good meat and I thought if it's good enough for lions, it must be good enough for me.

We were also fortunate to have a trained butcher from the army Catering Corps with us and he made short work of turning the animal into venison steaks and chops. We all ate our gazelle steaks and set about getting drunk. It didn't take long for someone to start singing. 'I zigga zumba zumba zumba, I zigga zumba zumba eh, hall them down, you zulu warrior hall 'them down you zulu chief chief chief, chief, ah zigga zumba zumba zumba ah zigga zumba zumba eh.' The song in itself sounds like something the Masai would sing. We could see them getting in to the mood, banging their spears on the floor. One of the soldiers stood on a table and started stripping off, something soldiers did all the time. What was the highlight of the night was when we were singing, one of the local men decided to get into the spirit of the dance. He had been drinking our beer and whiskey and was obviously a little drunk. He had us all in stitches after he jumped on the table, threw off his red blanket type poncho and was dancing naked on the table. It was a good laugh that night as one of the sappers also gave us a laugh as he had a puff adder in his sleeping bag and everyone was too pissed to do anything, so everyone just laughed when he said there was a puff adder on his bed.

The next day we were given the day off, as we had been working solid for six weeks. The Army doesn't normally stop

FLASHBACKS

because it is Sunday or any other day. But they said we could have the day off as the camp was more or less finished. The main regiment would be out after Christmas, to start the main job of road and bridge building. We had stripped out the radio equipment from one of the two Land Rovers and made it a ground station, giving us a spare Land Rover.. We kept that to ourselves, although we did let the Engineers borrow the Land Rover a couple of times. As such we were in the middle of the Kenyan bush and we had a Land Rover, which meant one thing to me and my mate Derek. We could become explorers again and not only did we have a day off, we had a land rover for our safari. We didn't know which way to head so we decided to follow the river. We then went along some tracks that looked roadworthy trying to make sure we could remember our way back. We followed the river for a bit, we would have looked a right pair of pricks if there had been anyone around to see us. I was wearing swimming trunks, army boots with puttees, sort of bandages wrapped around the tops of the boots. I had my webbed belt around my waist which contained my water bottle, with my machete in my right hand. I changed our names, I was now known as Tarzan and Derek was Jane.

After a couple of hours of following the river, I said to Jane, 'Do you know where we are?' He said 'yes', but I knew he didn't have a clue. We knew we had definitely gone wrong when we saw the next sign which said you are now in Uganda. Oops or words to that effect; we knew we were in trouble if we got caught. The guy in charge of Uganda was a self-imposed dictator called Idi Amin and If we got caught by his troops we would be in trouble. It might not have been so bad if we had uniforms on, but we laughed at the thought of a couple of corporals out of the British Army being paraded on the Ugandan news, in swimming trunks. What a pair of pricks we would have looked, suffice to say we did an about turn and tried to follow our nose to get back to civilisation. We knew roughly how many miles we had come, as you have to fill out a form in the army if you use a vehicle, so we knew we had come roughly fifty miles.

We spotted a giraffe walking across our path. I said to Derek, 'I know where we are.' He asked how, I told him that was the giraffe we saw when we set off. I also told him, I had just seen a sign for Narok and as such we would be okay as we knew the road from the trading post. I believe the road we were then travelling on had been built by the sappers, in a previous year.

As Kenya was part of the Commonwealth, our government supported them in such ways, building roads and bridges. I think the Kenyan government were on to a good thing, they would not only get new roads and bridges built by the British Army. They would charge the British government tens of thousands of pounds, for a squadron of Engineers to be in Kenya for six months.

The bridge the Engineers were building was manufactured in Italy. I believe that cost another hundred thousand pounds, which may not sound a lot now, but it was quite a lot then. The bridge itself was shipped to Kenya by a container ship, it was sent to the port in Mombasa. There it would be loaded onto low loaders and transported the four hundred miles to where we were. So along with the expense of all us soldiers

FLASHBACKS

being in Kenya for six month and the cost of the bridge. I guess the cost to the British taxpayer would be around half a million pounds. The Kenyans were the smart ones, getting paid for a gift, still that was politics and I was just a mere Lance Corporal, enjoying being in a Tarzan film.

We managed to get back to base camp before nightfall, roughly at the same time as a Major from another engineer unit. His name was Major Henry something and apparently he was a bit of a climber. Apparently he had climbed Everest and although his unit was in Kenya primarily to make maps, he also planned to climb Kilimanjaro. He did ask for volunteers as there would be some vacancies, nearly everyone volunteered.

His unit had arrived along with the main party of our regiment. So our camp swelled to its full capacity over the next few days. The bridge building started and that first day, it was all hands to the pumps. I had worked with the Royal Engineers all over the world, be it in Northern Ireland, where they would build barriers or in Central America, where they built the camp in Belize. The sappers in Kenya were no different to the engineers I had worked with around the world, a quality set of blokes. They cracked on working together and by the end of that first day they had built a temporary Bailey bridge across the river. It was impressive, what I didn't understand was why they didn't just leave the Bailey bridge across the river. I was told that the Bailey bridge was worth more than the bridge they were building and the fact that it could be dismantled would mean the Masai would probably take it apart. There was some urgency at the early stages as they had to get the foundations in for the main bridge, before the rainy season started. As I had managed to dispose of my shithouse duties by then, we concentrated on our main job, providing communications to the Engineers. The Sappers got stuck in to building the access road up to the bridge, whilst another team were digging the foundations for the bridge.

I spoke to the sapper who was in charge of one of the bulldozers. I told him I had a track licence from my time with the Desert Rats and as such would he let me have a drive of his machine.

'Yes no problem Corporal.'

I told him my name was Mick as he showed me the basic controls for the shovel and the controls for driving it. They did not look much different to the controls on the armoured personal carriers that I had initially learned to drive. The bulldozer seemed to have a mind of its own and it seemed to pull away much quicker than the only other track vehicles I had driven. I drove it over to our communications tent to show off to our lads. What I forgot was, we had buried our coax cable a few inches under the ground, the coax cable being the cable that fed the signal from the antenna to the radio equipment. Having forgotten it was a couple of inches below the surface of the ground, I managed to rip it in half, doing a snow plough turn with the giant dozer.

The thing about our job is that everyone loves you when you can call up an air strike, or put on the world service in the middle of the jungle, to get the football results on a Saturday. But as soon as you tell someone you have lost communications, they normally go spare. Being second in command of the communications cell we had built, I gave the sapper his

FLASHBACKS

bulldozer back and went back to work. Alan the young signaller on duty came out of the tent and said he had lost communications. I told him to have a break and I would have a look what was wrong with the link.

Just my luck, the Commanding Officer comes over and wants to send a signal regarding the Mt Kenya climb. It wasn't a priority so I had time to blag it, but I did tell the CO that we had lost our Morse link to Cyprus. He was a bit abrupt and told me he needed to be able to communicate. I said, 'Very good Sir, I am working on it and will let you know as soon as the link is restored.' Alan had wandered off to watch the sappers digging away at the foundations for the bridge and I searched frantically for our spare coax, as I knew if I didn't find it we were in trouble. Luckily I found it, changed the old one and restored communications. Alan came back and I told him everything was okay and he could continue his shift. I went over with a copy of the signal I had just sent for the CO and told him everything was fine and that the message had gone. I couldn't miss an opportunity to gain smarty points and a nice trip to Nairobi, so I thought. I told the CO that the local Masai had stolen the coax lead and that was the reason, for the lost communications

'Well done Corporal,' he said. 'Bloody good show, young man. I told him I was just doing my job.

That night as I fell asleep, I had a flashback to a tour of duty in Northern Ireland. My job at that time entailed going out on patrol with the Commanding Officer of the Royal Green Jackets. I did that for half the tour and the other half was spent in the HQ building. My job whilst out with the Colonel was to

FLASHBACKS

provide communications to the other patrols and then send SITREPs (situation reports) back to the Ministry of Defence. It was frustrating for soldiers in Northern Ireland as you had to get permission from the MOD for anything you wanted to do.

My flashback was of the IRA preparing to ambush one of the regular night patrols made by the Green Jackets. The Green Jackets were in my opinion a great infantry battalion, as infantrymen they were the best, which was just as well, that night. Two IRA men were being watched as they set up an ambush from their stolen white Vauxhall Viva. The IRA men didn't realise the army had an observation post over looking them, watching their every move. There were two soldiers communicating their every move to the troops on the ground. The soldiers could clearly see the two men had weapons and were obviously waiting for a patrol to open fire on. I wasn't part of the actual ambush as we parked up around the corner, we arrived as it finished, so I just saw the end result. There were a few patrols surrounding the ambush site and the outcome wasn't good for the two IRA men. The white Vauxhall Viva looked like a large Dalmatian with all the black bullet holes that were in the vehicle after the ambushers themselves were ambushed. Surprisingly only one of them died at the scene, the other would die later in the Royal Victoria Hospital. I believe the flashback was because I had been watching a lot of zebra running around. The black and white stripes had turned into the black bullet holes on the white Vauxhall. The thoughts of the black and white turns the flashback red as I remembered the blood splattered bodies of the IRA men inside the vehicle.

FLASHBACKS

As normally happens with flashbacks, you go from one to another and you keep going until you awaken covered in sweat. I jumped awake and started to remember what had been going on in my mind and what had happed prior to the flashback. I realised it was to do with the fact we had lost communications that day due to my negligence. I then remembered another time in Germany, when I was meant to send a flash message, which is a message you have to pass immediately. I learned a lesson the hard way as I didn't pass the message immediately, which got me two weeks in jail. I didn't enjoy the two weeks in jail but it did teach me a lesson and I believe it made me a better operator and soldier. After that I concentrated on my job and made sure I did everything by the book. Being in communications you have to deal with a lot of secrets although they don't always call them secret or top secret. They call them something else, a bit like James bond for your eyes only. If it is an operational message, being in Northern Ireland, we had to use a certain code. If it was something more delicate like a senior rank molesting another soldier, as had happened in the past. That would be sent as a delicate message, which also had a code. I remembered the day after the ambush the Colonel wanted me to send a message with regards to another IRA man. He asked me to send it with a secret heading, something similar to, for your eyes only. I informed the CO that such a message could only be sent or received by a qualified signaller, which I was. However to send such a message you have to first send a message saying you want to send a for your eyes only message, or a delicate text. The other end of the communications link would then need to get a signaller, with the ability to accept such a message. Then the two people receiving and sending the message would be able to confirm who they were by using another code, it was all a bit hush hush.

The Colonel came in that day and said, 'Send a for your eyes only message to the MOD.' They wanted to follow an IRA man wherever he went and that included any house he went into. For that reason they needed clearance from Whitehall, the Ministry of Defence. I told the Colonel I could send the message as a flash message, but could not send it as he requested and once again, I tried to explain about the clearance required on both sides of the link.

He said, 'Don't be stupid man and do as you're told.'

I said, 'I am sorry sir but you cannot do that.'

He said, 'Do as you are told or I will have you thrown in jail.' I sent the message as he requested, before it had finished the alarm bells went off and the message was jammed. The other operator telling me I could not send such a message without prior clearance.

I told the Colonel, 'I'm sorry Sir but they won't accept it.' He told me to try again, he ordered me to send it again, which I did under duress. Once again it stopped and I told the Colonel I could send it flash which would do the same thing, but he believed he was right. I took it on myself to remove the code for your eyes and made it a flash message, which has to be delivered within fifteen minutes.

Within the fifteen minutes we had clearance to follow the IRA man and that part of the job went well and he was caught. The other side of the coin was the Colonel got pulled over the

FLASHBACKS

coals and was given a ticking off about forcing me to send the message with a secret heading. He came down to the office and asked how a Corporal could have more power than a Colonel. I went on to tell him about the Official Secrets Act and as a Lance Corporal, I had been obviously vetted before I joined the army. Being attached to the Air Force as a Forward Air Controller I had worked at Strike Command, which at the time was somewhere down south. It was all quite hush hush and the headquarters were underground with an armed Snowdrop (RAF Policeman) on the entrance. I had gone down there with some SAS signallers and we all had unescorted badges, yet a Major who went to have a look around had to be escorted. He was more respectful to me after that and we got on well and he turned out to be a bit of a hero of mine. I could see why his men respected him, as he had the humility to accept he was at fault and not make me out to be an idiot, which he could have done being the boss.

My flashback and daydreaming over the next day in Kenya, the Colonel I had impressed, told me he would put me on the list for the Kilamanjaro climb. He did say, his main task was to get the bridge built before the rainy season started, otherwise it would have been a washout (excuse the pun). The foundations were going okay after a couple of weeks but there was a problem with the bridge; not the bridge itself, rather the transport bringing the bridge from Mombasa. It was being transported by the Kenyan equivalent of Pickford's, which was basically three trucks, all of which were about twenty five years old. In those days we didn't have mobile phones or even phones on the street, well not in that part of Kenya. That being

FLASHBACKS

the case, if a lorry broke down on the tracks, not only was it difficult for another vehicle to get passed, the drivers would sit in their lorry and wait until someone came or they were not reported as arrived. Because it was so slow getting from A to B through the bush, a lorry may take three days to get from Mombasa to the Mara. They would have overnight breaks firstly in Nairobi and then in a place called Nakuru.

The main part of the whole job as far as the Kenyans were concerned, was that it was their job to transport the bridge from Mombasa to the site at the Mara river. The commanding officer of the engineers was getting more frustrated all the time. He reminded me of Alec Guiness in *Bridge over the River Kwai*, except this was the bridge over the River Mara and it wasn't a film. He sent for me and explained what was happening, he then sent me off with Staff Sharp, the helicopter pilot. We were to fly to Mombasa, following the roads and tracks, taken by the Kenyan transporters. We were to look for any of the Kenyan vehicles carrying the bridge and check to see if they had broken down anywhere. I would then use the man pack radio to communicate their position. After we had flown the whole road to Mombasa and back it was obvious that there was no problem with the transport up to Nairobi. The main problems seemed to happen between Nairobi and Nakuru. The lorry drivers would stop overnight in Nakuru, so I suggested that if we had a communication point in Nakuru, we could then confirm as and when a Lorry had arrived or departed. We would also have a better idea as to which road the lorry was on and if it was broken down.

When we got back, I reported to the CO and gave him my ideas. I told him the only safe place we could set up a

FLASHBACKS

communication post, would be in Nakuru. We were given permission to go Nakuru to have a look around. It was amazing as the people there had never seen a helicopter up close. We landed in a field near to the hotel. There was an African Haulage Company lorry camped up in the village, for the night. It was decided that me and a private would be based there for 3 weeks until the bridge was completely delivered. Our job was to communicate with Mombasa and Nairobi, so as soon as a lorry left one of the locations, we would send the message informing the commanding officer the rough location of the vehicle at any one time.

We were booked in to the Pivot Hotel, which was basically a doss house, used by lorry drivers, but it was the only place we could stay. We were followed all the time in Nakuru, mainly by young nubile Kenyan women who were quite gorgeous. Having mainly just been watching Masai women walking around the camp at Mara, it was nice to see more normal women. I had only been there a couple of days when a gorgeous girl called Mitingani started following me around. She was about eighteen and had a gorgeous body. We had some of our civilian clothes with us and it was thought we should wear them rather than uniform. We had to check in every four hours during the day and pass on the situation report with regards to each lorry. After we had done our job our time would then be our own. Mitingani and I got friendly and the second night there I had a drink with her. I noticed she was wearing the same tatty blouse she had on the first day I saw her. After a few drinks we went up to my room and I gave her a red and white Ben Sherman shirt, it was a couple of years old. You would have thought I had just bought her a house if she had been an English girl. She was so pleased that she decided to take all her clothes off and try the shirt on, rather like a pyjama top. What followed later was even better as you can imagine.

The three weeks went quickly and although the trucks were still breaking down, we at least, were able to get to them within a few hours. That enabled us to get the bridge to the Mara, without any more dramas. I was sad to leave Nakuru to return to base camp and I missed Mitingani. I kissed Mitingani goodbye and gave her all my shirts except for one and she still seemed over the moon; the Kenyans are beautiful people and she was one of the best. They had sent a Land Rover from the Mara River with my mate Derek to collect us. We had arranged with the Kenyan army to fill up our vehicles in a place called Gilgil. We stopped off there to get some fuel and me and Alan went for a walk around the camp. It was quite obvious that the Kenyan army rank structure was not based on anything but the strongest guy would get promoted. As there were different tribes throughout Kenya there was a lot of rivalry, a bit like the Welsh, Irish, Scottish and English if you like, but really nasty with it.

We were stood outside the guard room and a voice shouted, 'Hello English.' It was a prisoner putting his head through the bars and asking for a cigarette.

I said, 'Sure mate'; after all he was a soldier and we are all soldiers, even if we were different. The guy spoke pretty good English and it turned out he was from a village near Nakuru. I asked him how long he was in jail for and what had he done wrong. He told me six weeks, I thought the guy must have done something pretty bad to get six weeks in jail. He said, he had been on manoeuvres near his village, which he had not seen for nine months. In Kenya, the soldiers had to do two years in the army national service and they didn't get leave. He went on to tell us, he had been camped up for the night and he knew he was only ten miles from his village. He had decided to run to his village to see his family. He hadn't been given permission but had decided he could get back before they moved out in the morning, so he had effectively gone absent without consent. He got back in time as his unit were still in the area they had camped up for the night. He told his troop Corporal that he had been to see his family and apparently the guy shopped him. He had been missed on a head count and as the corporal was from a different tribe, they didn't get on, so basically he just waited to get him.

I remembered back to when I went absent, when my twin ended up in the mental hospital and I had stayed there with him those three days. I got off with it because the Major in charge had a schizophrenic brother too and more or less said I did the right thing. The poor Kenyan soldier had really not done anything wrong in my mind. We were just passing the time of day with him when the some Kenyan Army Corporal came over and shouted at the guy in prison. He looked a right mean bastard; he would have got a good hiding from the rest of us in the British army for what he did. I told him to piss off and not be an arse hole, he shouted something in Kenyan and I just said, '*Jambo*' (hello). I believed the prisoner's story as he seemed quite intelligent and that would also probably get up the nose of this mad moronic Corporal who was in charge. I

FLASHBACKS

stood my ground and lit up another fag outside the prison whilst waiting for Derek to return from refuelling. I waited for the moronic Corporal to leave and then threw my fags and a lighter through the cell window. The guy shouted thank you and then we left.

Back to the Mara River, the bridge was well on its way when we got back to the camp. I couldn't believe how far it had progressed in the three weeks. The main part of the structure was up and by way of a bit of a jolly the pilot from the Army Air Squadron decided he would fly underneath the bridge; he was a nutter who had done quite a lot with Special Forces. He flew the Sioux helicopter under the bridge with a couple of feet above him to the bridge and a couple of feet below him to the river, in fact if a hippo had popped its head up they would have both been for the chopper so to speak. Apparently it was a bit of a dare and he only did it because the CO had been dropped off in Nairobi for some sort of chat with the Kenyan authorities. The stunt did look amazing, It was the sort of thing I would have done had I been a pilot.

The bridge was progressing nicely and we were back to safari one day, one day off and one day doing the communication business. We had been given the job of dealing with the messages for Major, the guy who was in charge of the Mt. Kenya climb; he was big pals with another army explorer, I better not name.

Running alongside the climb were the Royal Engineer map makers, as you have to justify being there. The climb was secondary so it was done under the pretext of making maps. Because of my good work in securing the communications for

FLASHBACKS

the CO and the transport job in Nakuru, I was given the chance to climb Kilimanjaro.

As we had a couple of days off, a mate of mine decided to go and have a better look at the mountain. We borrowed some jerry cans and took enough fuel to last; as we were more or less self-sufficient in Kenya we did what we wanted, to a degree. We drove out but decided it was too far to do in the day, so we decided it was best that we waited for the climb to start. It was just as well as whilst we had been away for a few hours, messages were coming in of an accident on the mountain. The map makers from the Engineers had finished their bit and were coming back down the escarpment from Mount Kenya. The vehicles they had were similar to what we had in Kenya, the old bull nose three ton lorry. On the way up the escarpment, a lorry developed brake problems. The leader of the expedition had decided it was best to put a straight bar tow on the lorry and carry on up the mountain to the base camp.

As it was quite a trek to get to the base of the mountain, the lorry doing the towing also ended with brakes that were a little dodgy, having been pushing and pulling another vehicle. They effectively ended up with three vehicles up the mountain and only one with good brakes. As they had to send two vehicles back down mountain to collect more supplies, they decided to use the vehicle with good brakes to tow one of the other vehicles back down. A bar would be bolted to the back of the towing lorry and the front of the vehicle being towed. As such they put the vehicle with good brakes at the front and the one with poor brakes at the back with the straight bar tow. On reflection they should have put the one with good brakes

FLASHBACKS

at the back and waited for the guy in front to press his brakes. Hence when they saw his brake lights they could have braked at the same time. Sadly they didn't and half way down the escarpment the brakes of the front lorry went. With the weight of the other lorry pushing it, the front lorry slid over the edge of the escarpment. There were around fourteen men coming down the mountain and several died. The ones who survived had jumped out of their lorry as it rolled down the mountain, before exploding.

You have to take your hat off to the RAF at the time, as one of the men who survived the accident, needed a kidney machine to save his life. We were busy with all the messages and to cut a long story short, the RAF flew out a kidney dialysis machine to save the guy's life. His parents and the families of some of the other injured and dead servicemen were also on the flight.

With all the commotion of that day, I once again went in to flashback mode as I went to sleep that night, thinking about the poor guy who had been burnt. It took my bad dreams back to Ireland as I remember going to an incident where a man had been tarred and feathered. I believe it was something the IRA did to informers or anyone who they believed were informers. I couldn't help thinking about the cruelty of people as I also remembered being a boy soldier and not understanding what life was about. I had it in my mind the first soldier I knew of that had died in Ireland. I was only fifteen and a boy sergeant called Paul Genge had just left boy service and I believe he was just eighteen. He had just left the boys college, joined his unit and went straight to Northern Ireland, only to be murdered. My thoughts at the time were of how quickly you could leave

FLASHBACKS

training and be killed. Everyone who knew him from the college thought him a hero and they even named a cup after him the Paul Genge cup. To a lot of people he was a hero to die, but to us, it was like losing a brother and the thoughts of his parents were never far from our hearts.

In some ways the poor guy who had been tarred and feathered and murdered was a hero to someone. His death seemed sadistic, in the fact that you cannot believe a person could do such a thing to another human being. The young guy who had been tarred and feathered had three knitting needles in his stomach. I remember wondering at the time, if they pushed the needles through him before they tarred and feathered him or after.

Back in Kenya the upshot of the Sappers dying was that I wasn't going to climb Kilimanjaro, well not at that time anyway. It put a downer on the whole camp as some of the guys who died were known to the Sappers on the bridge. As engineers, they are all trained in the same college and consequently even though they go to different units, they still remember each other.

As with life in the army, you cannot dwell on the occasions when someone dies, you absorb it, get pissed and talk about whatever you knew about them and have a laugh. It was the only coping mechanism I ever understood as a soldier. To lose so many men in one go does have a bigger effect on your life as you can imagine you have to get really pissed.

My flashbacks were constant that night, as per normal with my flashbacks the link is what happens in the day. That day having lost several soldiers linked me to the first time I witnessed a loss of life, where quite a lot of soldiers died

FLASHBACKS

It was whilst on an exercise in Denmark, near to the Kiel Canal. It was a massive airborne exercise and we were part of it. There were airborne brigades from all over the world but mainly part of NATO as it was a NATO exercise. The drop zone was just past the canal and although I was part of the Armoured Brigade at the time, we were supporting the airborne. Basically the drop zone at night would be lit up by a yellow beacon. The pilots would use the beacon as a signal to put the green light on, for the Paratroopers to jump. Unfortunately that night, the person in charge of the canal didn't do his job and a ship with a yellow lit beacon went down the canal. The pilot of one of the Hercules transport planes carrying the soldiers mistook the beacon from the ship to be the beacon for the dropping zone. Twenty plus soldiers died that night, the ones that didn't realise they were jumping into the canal were drowned. They were pulled under the water with the weight of their kit and the weight of the wet canvas also dragged them under. The exercise was called off and we were able to go back to camp and get pissed. They were not all English but they were still soldiers, I was still only eighteen at the time and even by then I had already seen or been on an exercise where someone died.

It appeared that there were as many soldiers dying out of action as dying in action, as was the case in Kenya. I had to get it out of my mind, that night back at the base camp, the CO had said a few words about the incident and then we all got pissed.

The next day at the Mara, I woke up drained as I always did after a flashback. We had a month left to finish the bridge before the rainy season started, so everyone had to get stuck in so the days off were gone. In our spare time we did work on

FLASHBACKS

the bridge, be it painting or anything that we were asked to do. I was starting to think about going home as you always seem to do when you were coming to the end of something. Sadly I couldn't remember coming back from any big exercise without having lost someone.

With those thoughts and dreams I suddenly came back to the reality of my own situation. I was not in Kenya, I was in military hospital and I was still sat in front of the Doctor. I must have been waffling on, whether it was the drugs or maybe it was the fact that I was spending most of my days talking to the shrink or young John. I had no idea about time but I must have been in with the shrink a long time, he told me to go and have lunch. I knew I had been in hospital nearly five months by then, because it was Christmas and someone else had told me, I'd been in since August. I found out that I had had plastic surgery on my face, to sort out my face after an incident and that I had been on that ward for a couple of weeks.

I can only describe my life at that time, in hospital, as though I was having dental treatment every day. It was like every time I went to sleep or had a flashback, that time disappeared and was lost forever. I can best describe it by saying it was like being given gas at the dentist, that strange feeling you had as you wake up, not knowing who or where you are. It was only when someone shakes you, or speaks to you that you seem to come around.

I came around that day not knowing what had been real or if I had just been dreaming about speaking to the Colonel and Kenya. I didn't know if I had been put to sleep with drugs or I had just woken up from a sleep.

FLASHBACKS

What did seem real was that it was young John who was shaking me and talking to me, he was saying he was really tired. I could see, he looked tired as he asked me if I was going for a run around the rugby pitches. I said I would, to which he replied, he had been worried about me and missed me.

'I haven't been anywhere,' I told him. 'I have just been here talking to you.'

He told me he hadn't seen me for a few days, he didn't know where I had been. He'd asked the RAF nurse where I was and was just told not to worry .

I remembered vaguely about kicking off about something or someone, it couldn't have been the drugs as I was only taking them whenever I had to. Sometimes they would keep you back in the queue to make sure you had taken them and not put them under your tongue. They were designed to burn as that's what happened if you put them under your tongue too long. I didn't know or care at that point as though I had just come out of gas at the dentist. Things started to look clearer and I told John I would go for a run. He kept saying he had missed me as he thought I had got better and gone back to my unit. Because I wasn't there he had not talked to his Gran either as it was me, the communication man, that would always took him to find a phone. His Gran, as far as I knew she was the only person who cared about him.

I seemed to forget about my own situation when I was with John. I guess John was never a soldier, he joined like a lot of young guys did, to impress a girlfriend or for a bit of adventure. I remember I joined to get fed, as I remembered as a child going days without any food. In those days my mother said she had no money and we just accepted it. I think the shrink I was seeing was trying to put my being in hospital down to my childhood. I told him my childhood made me strong and whatever was wrong with me was something to do with the army. My childhood was tough mainly because my mother had problems, besides having to bring up six children on her own.

I went with young John as I knew for some reason John needed me more than I needed him. It wasn't just for the phone calls and that I was a Corporal and talked to him like a mate. It was something deeper and it was as though I was like a father to him, as he hadn't had a father, yet I was in my late twenties myself and had never had a father to call a dad. I did a few laps around the rugby posts and sat with my back against the post. I knew I hadn't been running for a while as I only managed four laps and I was knackered. John was at the other side with his back against the posts as normal, telling me that he had missed me, I said, 'Sorry mate I told him as I didn't even know where I'd been.'

I asked him if Rifleman Terry or the thick Scottish bloke out of the Black Watch had been giving him a hard time. He said the Scottish bloke was locked up in some jail after going home on leave for a long weekend, got drunk and smashed a bloke in the face with a pint glass.

'I didn't know he had it in him,' I told John. Funny enough my twin brother who is schizophrenic ended up in the local nut house in Sheffield as he had done something similar.

'Do you think we are schizophrenic Corporal?' he asked me.

FLASHBACKS

I told him, 'No John I know what psychos are like as my twin has been diagnosed all his life with it. I don't know what's wrong with me John and I only know you are tired, there is obviously something but I don't know what.'

It was then I told him about Rifleman Terry when I first saw that shrink and how I listened to the rifleman and I understood him and I knew where he was coming from. But I also knew that the shrink didn't have a clue, as I was confused why the shrink couldn't understand what the rifleman was on about as it was straight forward to me. That's why I couldn't be arsed talking to them, I told John, because they don't know what's happening with us because if they did they would be treating us rather than drugging us.

In some ways it reminded me of my twin brother when he was crying as a young man, locked up in a nut house. My poor twin, I thought, not only did they give him drugs to shut him up they fastened him down on a bed like Frankenstein and gave him electric shock treatment, I was there afterwards and I realised they were not treating him, they were erasing his brain. The sad thing at the time, I told John, I was absent without leave from the army and it was difficult to leave my twin getting abused by the so called doctors and nurses, more like Boris Karloff and Christopher Lee in some horror movie.

Young John listened as he always listened. It's as though I could tell him anything and he was always amazed or maybe he just liked me.

'I have missed talking to you Corporal.'

I said, 'For God's sake John you can call me Mick.'

He said 'Thanks Corporal,' 'While you have been away

FLASHBACKS

Rifleman Terry got discharged.'

I said, 'From the army?' He said, 'No he went back to his unit.'

Well that did give me some hope as I believed I had understood where the rifleman was coming from with his anger. I told John there were vast differences between the rifleman and me, for a start I had a brain.

John chuckled and I was pleased I could cheer him up by just taking him along with me and chatting. I remembered when I was on the plastic surgery ward, when I used to take my young para mate Paul to the pub. We put the world to right on those Sunday afternoon sessions in the local pub. I remember he was always happier when he was with me than with his Mum and Dad and family. It's as though as a soldier you can only fulfil life being with other soldiers. As and when you are taken away from being part of a military situation, you cease to accept things. Maybe it is the fact that you are brainwashed in training for two years and you become like a robot. It was as though you had a brain and then it got tuned, in my case for many years, into what I was. I don't ever believe I was afraid, or maybe I was afraid but too afraid to show it, was nearer the mark.

Maybe I needed to focus on my lack of feeling and why I wasn't afraid when I witnessed death. I was afraid afterwards when I realised what I witnessed, it scared me, but then I was too afraid to tell anyone later that I was afraid afterwards. As being a Corporal, I always had to show leadership and as such I wasn't allowed to be afraid. There was always something in me that gave me courage. I used to think it was my mother and I also thought it could be my twin brother. It was as though

FLASHBACKS

I had to be brave for the two of us. I had at least learned that I wasn't afraid when it came to the crunch, only afterwards, which as a soldier must be a good thing.

All these thoughts are flying through my mind at the same time as I am listening to John telling me how tired he is. I said, I am the one who is training. 'You have only been sat there mate, I am the brainwashed twat who has to keep running.'

I said, 'I'm glad Rifleman Terry has gone back to his unit,' as I thought he would get the chop from the army as he had lost control. I told John 'not like you and me mate, we are in total control of ourselves mate', he just laughed. With that John told me you have done a lot more than me Corporal, I wish I had been to somewhere like Kenya,' he said. 'I only came out of training and went to Ireland.'

'I didn't know I had been talking to you about Kenya John.'

He said, 'Since you came back on the ward we have been chatting and you were talking about Kenya and it sounded great, apart from the guys dying coming down the mountain.'

Sadly I had been in hospital all the time and I didn't realise how quick the time was going.

'It sounds bad Corporal but I am glad you are in hospital with me as I didn't like it when you were locked up or wherever they put you.' I truly didn't know where I had been.

I told John the last couple of weeks were just a blur and that I was pleased I could be there for him. I also said my aim was to get back to my unit, as it could not be doing my army career any good, being locked up in the nuthouse.'

I asked John if he had seen the RAF Corporal who confides

FLASHBACKS

in us, the guy who tells us what's happening. John told me that he believed the medic had been on leave for three weeks and that he would return tomorrow, Sure enough the next day I saw Corporal Crab, he wasn't a bad bloke for a crab, he said he couldn't talk to me at that present time but he would come over and talk to me later that evening, when the ward got quiet. He was good to me as I had been attached to the RAF. We had a bit in common and we were both the same rank, he told me that a lot of the guys in that ward were wankers and they just wanted out of the army. He said strangely enough the only two people on the ward he believed to be ill were me and John. He knew we were not putting anything on, unlike some of the guys trying to work their ticket out of the army.

I said, 'I don't want to leave the army, it's the only thing I have known from being fifteen and it's the only thing that gave me a life. Besides the deaths I had witnessed I had great times,' I told him, 'especially with you crabs, when I was attached to the RAF it was like being on holiday as a soldier, nice food, spoken too, like you are someone and shown respect. I guess you get a brighter type of bloke in the RAF,' I told him.

He said, 'You are quite smart Corporal, if you are smart, you can recognise other smart people.'

Anyway I said if I am so smart why is it I couldn't remember where I have been the last few weeks. I told him, 'I only know I have been locked up the last few weeks because John told me and he said he had missed me.'

'The RAF corporal said I shouldn't be telling you this, I am going to as you need to know, I don't think you realise how ill John is and you don't think that you are ill in any way. The fact

FLASHBACKS

is for the last three weeks, you have been back at your unit in Catterick. You were sent back to work as one of the two Corporals in charge of leadership troop.

I could not believe what he was telling me, I was sure he was having me on and he was going to tell me he was joking. I said I thought I had been locked up for kicking off as it was the last thing I remembered. He told me that was a few weeks ago and that I kept on insisting that I would be fine and I actually convinced the powers that be that I would be fine if I were able to get back to my unit and do my job. I asked him the obvious question as to how I got back to hospital if I had been returned to my unit. He started to tell me, initially they thought I was okay and although I was on some medication.

He told me about the time, I went in to the TV lounge where some of the potential officers were watching TV. It was midnight and apparently I told them, I had been laying in bed thinking about lots of things bad, sad and I had told them I had been praying. I told them of the lady in blue and white, surrounded by a halo of lights. As I had no one to tell I went across to the TV lounge and asked the guys to come and look at it. When they went in to my room, they found nothing there. I still felt the calm and peace in my mind and body. He asked me what I had been praying about and I told him that I prayed my mother and brother were well, I prayed for the families of all the servicemen I had known that had been killed up to that point and I prayed that there must be a better life. I said it was like I found out that you only realise about life through suffering and my life had had a lot of that, but I never thought I was affected by those things. After all it wasn't me who died and it

FLASHBACKS

wasn't me who was cruel. I could never tar and feather someone or leave anyone like young John to suffer without talking to him. I told him I give a shit about people, especially my comrades as I know soldiers suffer with soldiers because that's how it goes. You are in it together, whatever it is, and when you come out of it, God willing you are okay. I know that doesn't happen all the time and that's why I prayed I guess.

The medic said, he didn't know I was a religious person. I said, 'I am not religious, I just know that there is a God. That night I knew whatever it was that came to me, was real and I lost all fear after I had seen that vision.'

'Well,' he said, 'you had lost all fear Mick because a couple of days later you were found in the centre of the motorway, walking towards the oncoming traffic. You obviously were not in a good state of mind as that is not the actions of a sane person. He told me I had a 9 mm pistol on me and as the police talked to me I apparently pointed it at my head and pulled the trigger. The police realised the gun was empty and they grabbed me and after locking me up for a few hours I was returned to hospital.

When he told me that, I remembered a 9mm pistol, it was a Browning and I had it tucked in my trousers at the back. It was a replica I had obtained from somewhere and when arrested I told the police I was returning to Belfast from Lisburn. They knew instinctively that I was obviously mentally ill and being in uniform, they knew I was a soldier. I was going on and on about the time in Northern Ireland and how the army always used Ford Escorts and minis. I was telling the police that the weapon was for my own protection.

FLASHBACKS

Can I be dreaming?' I asked the RAF Corporal.

'No mate, what I have told you really happened and the boss wasn't sure about whether you should have been sent back to your unit as he thought maybe it was too soon because we had not really found out what made you flip in the first place. But we do know one thing, it is real, and you are very ill. John seems to have pepped up since you came back anyway so at least that's a good thing. If you could, we would like you to keep an eye on John as he seems to confide in you.'

I told him, 'It probably helped John that Rifleman T went back to his unit and the Black Watch twat wasn't about, as they picked on John.'

He said, 'They are no longer around, so it won't happen again. I asked him if they had gone back to their units?' and he said, 'Yes.' I told the Corporal that I have known about being afraid after incidents, but I hadn't known real fear like this before; the fear of not knowing what has been happening to me and what was going to happen to me in the future.

He said, 'Just let's concentrate on getting better and take one step at a time.' He told me not to worry about things as it is normal for the mind to switch off or blank out something that is traumatic. He explained something about the brain pushing trauma into a part of the brain that will help to keep your mind safe.

I said, 'I know,' as I had been in many a traumatic situation that had freaked me out.

The Corporal, or should I say nurse, asked me if I wanted to talk about it. Just as he said that, young John returned, he always came for a chat at night. It's was as though it was my

FLASHBACKS

job to tell John a bed time story of my exploits. I asked John if I should talk to the Corporal about Kenya.

John said, 'What about those guys getting killed.' The nurse asked me if those guys in Kenya getting killed was the thing I found traumatic, I told him on a scale of one to ten on what I found traumatic, the incident in Kenya was about a three or four. I wasn't responsible in any way for what happened to those men, so although I felt sad, I didn't feel guilt. Had I been there when the accident occurred, I may have felt different. I did feel sadness for the families of the dead as I had dealt with that situation many times.

'So what was it about Kenya that you found traumatic?' asked the Corporal, and John said, 'Please tell us Mick.'

I started to tell them something that did affect me, but not about soldiering, just the fact that I was trapped and I could not fight my way out. I had never really enjoyed flying, especially in RAF transport planes, the Belfast and the Hercules mainly as they were in my mind the scariest. I remembered coming in to land in Akrotiri and the plane being struck by lightning. Also the fact the plane going into darkness for a few moments also scared me. At that time, I would not say I had a phobia about flying, I was just a little apprehensive.

'That's understandable,' said the Corporal, 'but you carried on so obviously it was not a problem.'

'It wasn't a problem because, I was more afraid of telling someone I was afraid, than actually facing what was worrying me. I said it was like when someone shoots at you, you are more afraid to say you're afraid than shoot back, so in some ways you are being forced to do something against your better judgement. I would want to run away from the danger, which is to flee, but in a situation like the Belfast getting hit by lightning, I could not fight or flee to escape the danger. I know that there is a strange connection to killing, being killed or seeing someone killed. They are all things that go against our better judgement, so doing either one creates fear and the wish to run. I could still fight or flee at the time but what happened when I left Kenya was real fear as I could not fight or flee, I was trapped.'

John asked me if I had been attacked by something, if not what was it that had made me scared.

I said, 'I will tell you as I have never really talked about it, but I was afraid I was going to die that night.'

I was mainly telling John as I had been talking to him about Kenya and the nurse just listened. I had just spent my last couple of days in Kenya down at the barracks in Kahawa. The bridge had been finished, the major still climbed his mountain and as we had been the advance party out to Kenya we were to be the first out of Kenya. Being part of an air portable brigade we had to prepare our vehicles for the return trip to Britain. Our vehicles were easily recognised as we had red hands painted on the doors of our land rovers.

John asked me if we put red hands everywhere we went, I said, 'No we put mushrooms.' He didn't understand about the mushrooms. I said we only had red hands on the doors of our Land Rovers but it was a Squadron thing about the mushrooms. So that's why if you ever went anywhere in the world, you might see mushroom shapes, normally made out of red plastic tape and the shape of the mushroom is visible (the idea was you had to stick it somewhere you would find it difficult to get off).

I told them I remembered visiting a bar in Rabat Malta in the middle of nowhere and it had a ceiling that was about eight metres high and it had four fans on the ceiling whizzing around. We looked up at the ceiling and each one of the fans had a red mushroom on them whizzing around. We had a laugh with the owner as he told us about the soldiers who had been in the bar some ten years ago. They got drunk, then built a pyramid in the main bar area, using the tables and chairs to enable them to reach the fans. They ran out of tables for the last part, one man got on the other mans shoulders on the top table, to finish the job.

He said, 'No one will stack the tables to take them down,' and now he enjoyed seeing them as he liked the British.

As for the red hands, I went on to tell them about a NATO exercise we did in Verona, Italy. Because all our vehicles had the red hand motto, the Italians thought we were communist and didn't realise we were British, although we also had Union Jacks on the bumpers of the vehicles. I remembered Italy at that point as when we drove through the towns, the old people would raise their fists and shout Mussolini. I didn't know the significance at the time but I did later, as I didn't know Italy had been communist. I knew I was starting to talk about something other than Kenya and the return trip home. It was as though I was trying to avoid bringing the trip into my mind. I carried on talking about Italy, I went on talking, I told them how I associated Italy with my father. It was just a coincidence I was in a place that I knew my father had been in the war. I remember I was four or five when he told me stories about being in the

FLASHBACKS

army in Italy. I remember the exercise we were on in Italy stretched from Verona in the north down as far as Florence in the south. On the exercise, I found myself at Monte Casino and I saw all the British gravestones. The British war cemetery was just north of Florence. I remember thinking at the time, my father was here with the 17/21st Lancers, a light armoured regiment; a regiment that was still in existence. I was walking through the graveyard and then I saw the graves of a few 17/21st Lancers, with the skull and cross bones of their cap badge embedded on their tombstones. These men may have known my father and vice versa. I didn't know much about my father except that he came back from the war mentally scarred and married another mentally scared person, my mother, who had lost most of her relations fighting in the Greek resistance.

'Of course that was memories rather than flash backs,' I told the nurse and John.

It was the nurse who interrupted and told me, I was talking like I did with the Colonel, I was avoiding talking about what was really bothering me. He said the only way to overcome my problems were to face them and once again asked me what happened in Kenya that affected me, I told him it wasn't so much in Kenya more after leaving. We had already air prepped our vehicle for the seventeen hour flight back from Nairobi to RAF Lyneham, so I just drove the vehicle on to the Hercules or C130 as they were known. The Loadmaster is the RAF equivalent of a British Airways engineer and it was his job to ensure the plane is loaded correctly and that involved chaining the Land Rovers down to the floor of the plane. He also was the guy responsible for the opening and closing of the main doors, including the

FLASHBACKS

ramp. In short he was responsible for everything that happened within the plane. After driving our land rover on to the plane, my mate and I walked back down the ramp. We headed back to the hanger, which was effectively the waiting room for transit passengers. We were sat there for ages waiting for the loadmaster to give us the nod, to board the Hercules. There were about fifty of us waiting to board and you could tell everyone was a bit anxious. By that time it was two in the afternoon and we should have left an hour previous. Of course it doesn't really bother the RAF if they don't leave on time as it's not like civilian flights. We waited for another half hour, then along came the Loadmaster and told us to board. I wanted to make sure I got a seat up the front, near where our Land Rover was chained down, as I wanted to be the first out of my seat. It was always a rush to get to the best place to sleep, which was on the top of the canvas in between the frames of the Land Rovers.

The Hurclules c130

FLASHBACKS

Unlike British Airways aircraft, the only window you can see out of in a Hercules, is situated about six feet above your head, like the porthole of a ship. So you can only see out of the window by standing on the net seating of the aircraft or climbing onto the Land Rovers to look out. At that time I just wanted to get up in the air and out of that net seat. You can see all the cables and nuts and bolts and everything that operated the wings or ailerons. When the plane moved, you could see something inside the plane moving. It enabled the Loadmaster or Engineer to go to a spot if there was a problem occurring with any part of the plane. We had only been flying for about twenty minutes and we were still waiting for the Loadmaster to tell us to unfasten our seat belts, when the plane dropped out of the sky for want of a better word. I thought I was a goner at the time. But that turned out to be a bit of a false alarm, not that the plane was okay. The Loadmaster came out of the cockpit with his little hammer.

He said, 'Not to worry lads.' The reason we had dropped so quickly was because we were working our way up to twenty six thousand feet and we were at around eighteen thousand feet, when the alarms came on. He said the pressurisation unit on the aircraft had failed and if we had been any higher than we may have been in trouble. He assured us that the pressurisation units on that particular military aircraft were triplicated and although it may have scared us, we did not need to worry.

He told us the bad news is, due to regulations we would have to return to Nairobi and check everything out. There was nowhere else for us to go on route and as such, the best thing

FLASHBACKS

was to return to Nairobi. To that end he informed us that the aircraft would be banking from left to right for the next ten minutes or so, as they had loaded enough fuel on the aircraft to get us to Oman. Oman was to be our first port of call to refuel and maybe pick up some special forces returning to England.

We were all cheesed off as we had already lost a few hours and it meant we were not going home. Although by that time, with my army career, I had a couple of hundred hours in Hercs, I had never been in one that ditched the fuel. I had my feet up against my own vehicle and as the aircraft started to bank, I started watching the chains that strapped the underneath of the vehicles to the floor of the aircraft. The first bank took the Land Rover onto one side, held by the chains to stop it sliding. With each bank of the aircraft, you could see one set of chains tense up, while the opposite chains went slack. You could feel and sense the strain on the chains as they held the Land Rover in situ, whilst the fuel was ejected out of the end of the wings.

You got a sense of relief when the plane banked the other way and if the chains snapped the guys sat on the opposite seats would get clobbered. It didn't take long for it to become your turn again and so it went on until the plane had ditched enough fuel out of the wings to enable it to land safely. That experience was a first, but I did learn that a plane has to get rid of spare fuel before it can land. We managed to land at RAF Eastleigh which was an old RAF Base in Kenya. I think they had landed there to be safe from the civilian airport.

John said, 'You must have crapped yourself Corporal.'

FLASHBACKS

I said, 'Not really mate, I was a bit apprehensive but I would not have said I was scared.'

After we had landed, we were still sat in our seats as the Loadmaster started to lower the ramp at the back so we could walk off. The pilot had shut down the engines and came down the little spiral steps from the cockpit of the aircraft. He was quite apologetic about having to return to Nairobi and said he was sure we would not have to stay there. He looked quite relaxed and seemed quite confident about his ability. He just seemed so laid back, which in some ways was reassuring.

The Loadmaster heard the pilot and looked at him and smiled. I thought they knew something we didn't know, but we were on the ground, so they must have done the job right. Once again we were sat around for another hour and a half. Eventually the Loadmaster came into the transit room, where we were all sat. He told us we would be leaving as soon as we refuelled. Apparently the problem with the pressurisation unit could not be resolved and had we been back in England we would not have flown. However as the unit that had malfunctioned had two back up units, we would be taking off and flying to Oman, where we would get the part repaired, prior to carrying on to England. He assured us we had nothing to worry about and to be extra safe we would not be flying at normal altitude. Just in case the pressurisation unit malfunctioned again, we would fly at a lower altitude, which would enable us to drop down to 10,000 feet as soon as possible.

I didn't know how much he was telling us, was what we needed to know or just bull shit, I knew I really wasn't paying attention. I just wanted to get on the plane and go home.

FLASHBACKS

Once again we boarded and although I was a little apprehensive, I had something or someone with me and I didn't seem to care. It was the same feeling of someone I had felt on many occasions from childhood. Whatever it was, I felt it was with me through all things that happened to me, not just as a child, a soldier, but in my everyday life. I only recognised it when I felt afraid and sure enough I stopped being afraid; it was like I didn't care what would happen as long as I could keep that feeling of not caring about what happened. I always kept the feeling so as such I didn't care, as my mother would sing to me all my childhood, *Que Sera Sera* (whatever will be will be). Thinking of my mother also reassured me, especially when thinking about the trauma she had suffered, growing up in Greece and fighting Germans.

I managed to relax with the thoughts of *Que Sera Sera*, going through my mind, on and on, maybe the thing that was in my mind and always looked out for me was my mother. She always did protect us, but this was more than my mother, it was something else keeping me safe, besides the thoughts of love I had for my mother.

With those thoughts, I felt the Hercules juddering as the four propellers started whizzing around. The noise was incredible and I could see through the porthole across from me, the smoke and the reflection of a propeller as it cut through the sunshine coming through the porthole.

'Here goes,' I thought, as the plane, once again started rolling down the runway. The fear I felt was also being blanked, once again the engines strained to pick up this massive piece of metal and launch us in to the air. My thoughts were of the

FLASHBACKS

hand of God as if God had an invisible hand made of an air pocket. The engines strained away for a few minutes or so and then this big hand lifted the plane onto a nice fluffy cloud. The engines stopped screaming, like most of the soldiers in the back of the Hercules as they struggled to be heard, above the noise of the engines.

The Loadmaster came around after a couple of hours and told us we can move around now and relax. He said we would be aiming for Oman and we should be there in several hours. I could see through the portholes the redness of the sun as it was going down. I wasn't sure of the time, but I decided I would hit the top of the Land Rover with my long serving sleeping bag, before any of the other guys flying home had the same idea. I scrambled up and as if by way of saying good night the Loadmaster turned the lights off inside the plane and all you could see was the little red warning lights that lit up the inside, enough to look around but not bright enough to stop you sleeping. I managed to fall asleep for a couple of hours and then woke up as it was starting to get warm on the top of the Land Rover. I decided to climb down, still half asleep, but was jolted in to complete awareness as once again the Hercules went into a dive. The Loadmaster was shouting at everyone to buckle up, at the same time rushing over to some sort of equipment under the wing, across from where we sat.

Alarms were going off everywhere and the little red lights that had been so relaxing were now flashing. The chains holding the Land Rovers down to the floor, were being tested fully as the aircraft dropped. As the plane dropped, you could see the chains, you could see they went slack as the springs of

FLASHBACKS

the vehicles bounced and then sprung back up yanking the chain like a tug of war rope, being slackened and pulled. Even with all the flashing and dropping, just to make sure we knew something wasn't right they put on this hideously noisy alarm, like a fire alarm. I didn't know what the Loadmaster was doing but I knew by his face that we were in some sort of trouble. The plane once again levelled off and started to descend, the Loadmaster resolved his problem and told us we didn't need to worry all was under control. Our position was that the pressurization unit had once again gone and we had to land as soon as possible. Whatever was wrong with the transport plane was maybe too shocking to tell us, but I did admire his cool and I just said, 'Thanks for letting us know Sarge.'

It was about midnight and we were certainly falling out of the sky faster than normal to land. The loud speaker on the aircraft came to life with the pilot saying, 'Unfortunately chaps we have a slight problem, but just relax and we will be landing shortly'. He went on to say, 'We have not been given permission to land but we will have to resolve that problem once the Hercules is on the ground.'

It was like listening to Douglas Bader in the battle of Britain film, only I was disappointed that our pilot didn't go 'tally ho, tally ho.'

My body was now electric, yet unbelievably calm and I just knew we would get down okay. I just accepted that in my mind and tried to relax a little. The plane kept dropping and dropping until we banged onto the runway. Having landed many times in those transport planes, I knew this was a heavy landing as my back jarred up to the back of my neck. Whilst we were still

FLASHBACKS

taxiing along the runway, the Loadmaster went to the rear of the aircraft and was lowering the ramp. It was dark but as soon as the ramp was half way down, there was a massive rush of warm air. It was like we had just been thrown into a fan oven.

We could make out some head lights going past us to the front of the aircraft. The pilot came on the blower once again, 'I am afraid we have had to land in the Yemen as it was too risky to try for Oman. We have been instructed to stay on the plane and await an escort. No one is to disembark until, myself or the Loadmaster instructs you to do so.'

At that point the only thought in my head was that I was never going to get home. I thought it cannot get any worse, I was about to find out that it could. The ramp was more or less down and we all stood up, eager to get off.

The pilot piped up again, 'I am sorry chaps we are in a communist controlled republic and at the moment they believe us to be a group of mercenaries here to kidnap their leader or whatever.' He said he had tried to explain to them who we were, where we had come from and where we were going, but they were having none of it.

The pilot told us, 'We have no alternative but to do what they ask and at the moment they want everyone on the aircraft to strip down to their underpants and bare feet, then when we are ready we have to put our hands above our heads and walk off in single file. We have been instructed to leave all our weapons on the aircraft and to walk off with a space between each man.'

With that, we all stripped down to our underwear and started walking off the plane. It did look like a bunch of

FLASHBACKS

captured mercenaries to tell you the truth. I am not talking about what we looked like, more the Yemeni military that had surrounded the aircraft. They formed a line along the route they wished us to walk. I realised then, we must be in the communist side of the Yemen, as their soldiers looked like something out of Pancho Villa or the Rio Grande. They had weapons with ammunition belts wrapped around their chests. They didn't look like an army; they looked more like bandits. The truth was it didn't matter what they looked like, at that moment we were their prisoners.

They took the air crew away; the pilot, navigator and engineer and we were all frog-marched into a greenhouse for want of a better word. It was, I believe, their transit room for prisoners and as such it was like a furnace with very little air. You could only just breathe as there didn't seem to be any ventilation in the room, just one window with bars about ten feet above our heads. We were all looking at each other and I started to laugh as it was so surreal. It became real after about thirty minutes, it was as though we were sat in a sauna, I couldn't believe it was so hot.

After an hour things outside may have be progressing a little better as a couple of guards came into the room, whilst the others kept their weapons pointed at us. They had decided to give us some water. By then we were all desperate for a drink, having been sweating profusely for the last hour. After the drink, the Loadmaster and the Engineer turned up to join us. They told us that the skipper was desperately trying to get some money authorised for the Yemenis. They had accepted that we had to land and that the plane had difficulties, but they still insisted that we leave as we should not have landed without permission. That was the case as far as we knew it, however they would give us our freedom, but money would have to be paid straight away and then we may be able to leave. I never really knew what went off with the MOD and the Yemeni government that night, but I do remember being allowed to leave.

The Loadmaster said, 'Better the devil you know, we would rather leave in a dodgy aircraft than be stuck somewhere, we may die from lack of air. Their army was a disorganised rabble, if what we had seen was the best of them. It took another hour or so to get the funds transferred. The pilot told us that we had enough fuel to get back, as to where back was I wasn't sure anymore. I had to give that thirty year old pilot credit as he was as cool as a cucumber.

Once again we were preparing to take off again, but this time I believe we had a problem with one of the engines, the pilot said he was going to shut it down straight after takeoff, according to the Loadmaster it was something they practiced all the time. The only other thing we had to worry about was how high we could fly and if the final pressurisation unit went, would we all die. The Loadmaster just laughed, the sort of laugh I had done when we had just been captured. The pilot told us we would not be flying at normal height and that we would be heading up the Red Sea towards the Mediterranean. I wasn't sure what he said about directions as I was more interested in getting away from the Yemen.

We all got settled in the aircraft, if not just a little apprehensive, especially when our cool pilot came on the loud speaker. His exact words were that we would be doing an

FLASHBACKS

overload take off and if we didn't get off the first time, we would be staying put. Having done so many take offs in Hercules transport planes I had a good idea as to how long it would take us to get up. The aircrafts engines were revved up and off we went. You could feel the pressure on the engines as it tried to lift off. It went up a little at the front then down slightly. Then with a mighty roar it started to lift after what seemed an eternity. I would like to say I was still cool about our situation but, like everyone on board the aircraft, the anxiety was showing on their face. Then the relief as the aircraft got in to the night sky, it was still dark and you could see the reflection of a light in the porthole window.

The next hour or so went slowly. I couldn't sleep, I just kept thinking about what we had been through. It didn't make sense. I started to wonder if we were involved in some sort of SAS exercise as I knew they had a troop stationed out in Oman. Maybe we had been used as some sort of exercise they would be involved in. I was busy day dreaming about such thoughts, when the alarms went off again on the Hercules. This was serious, I thought, as you could see what looked like flames out of the porthole against the night sky. The plane went dark again and it was definitely a fire in one of the engines. We were dropping down again, the Loadmaster came rushing down from the cockpit and climbed up to some sort of lever that he pulled which seemed to extinguish the fire.

The pilot came on the tannoy telling us all to strap in and we would level off shortly, he said, 'We have problems at the moment, but we are okay.' I could tell by his voice that we were in trouble.

FLASHBACKS

I was starting to wonder if I was going to die, when once again, the pilot piped up. 'We are going down and we will be making an emergency landing in Athens all being well.' Thanks for that, I thought, but I felt calmness, once again coming over my body. For some reason that I don't know to this day, something made me feel safe. Apparently we were about ten minutes away from Athens. It was after the pilot said we were landing in Athens, it was as though I knew we were going to be okay, I couldn't die in Athens as it was where my mother came from and her family were there. Once again I could see what I thought were flames out of the porthole. It was dark still and we were coming down faster than I had ever experienced in a Hercules. Everyone was told to bend over and adopt a crash position. I didn't. Instead I told the guy at the side of me that we would be okay. He did look a little sheepish, I felt sorry for him as I could not think anything other than we were going to be okay. The fact that the airport in Athens was only a matter of a couple of miles from the sea meant that we would either go into the sea or land. I could feel the land beneath the plane although I could not see out. The pilot told us to brace as we were a minute or so from landing.

'It may be quite a heavy landing,' were his last words. I knew we were coming in fast and I could now see reflections from the runway as we were coming down. I could see blue lights flashing and reflecting against the red and yellow light, which I believe was another fire on one of the engines, together they made a sort of purple colour.

With an almighty bang, the plane hit the runway, bounced a little and then banged in again. On the second bang the rear

FLASHBACKS

door ramp was being lowered. An officer sat on my left, leapt out of his seat and started running towards the ramp. I thought what a wanker he was trying to get off the plane first.

The Loadmaster told him that he should not be moving until he was told to do so, to which the captain said, 'I was just getting to the entrance to ensure everyone got off okay.'

The Loadmaster said, 'That's my job sir and I would like you to do as I say on the aircraft.'

We weren't out of the woods yet as we were being followed down the runway with fire engines and ambulances. The plane managed to come to a halt and sure enough that captain was the first off and in his rush he smashed a bottle of whisky as he jumped down from the ramp. I could have used a drink at that time. I was relieved, although I never thought of myself as being scared at that time. Like everything I did as a soldier, I never really felt scared at the time, it was always afterwards. That plane coming down was part of the jigsaw that is, and was, my life. Whatever destiny had been planned for me started from that point after the crash landing in Athens.

Both the RAF Corporal Nurse and young John were astounded at my story. They couldn't believe I was not scared. I told them it was because of my mother; I felt her with me and also something else but I didn't know what it was at the time. I knew I was meant to go to Athens and how pleased I was when I found out it was Athens. We were taken to a hotel in Athens and told we would be staying there until we could get a flight home. The next morning we were briefed that we would be staying in Athens for at least a week. I believe the powers that be knew we had been through something of an ordeal and they didn't want us arriving back at RAF Lyneham with all our families being there. The families were told at the last minute that we would not be back for another week.

Having been away for six months, I was wondering what my daughter would look like. Of course prior to that I had only seen her for about six months out of the nearly three years she had been alive. In those days I could return from one operation, be back a week and then off on another jolly for a couple of months.

I certainly didn't mind when they had booked us into the Apollo Palace Hotel in Athens. They gave us a few thousand drachmas at the time and basically said to relax. The idea was that there was a transport plane on its way back from Hong Kong in a week or so and we would be getting on that if they could not fix the plane we had arrived on. Apparently the plane that was going to Hong Kong would be dropping off in Athens with a team of RAF Flight Engineers, who would fix the plane and we would get on it to get home as soon as possible. Either way I didn't care, I had decided to find my mother's family. I knew her only surviving brother lived in Athens and I knew he had nine daughters.

I got permission from my boss at the hotel, I explained about my mother coming from Greece and that I had family in Athens. He gave me permission to look for them and to that end I just had to call the hotel twice a day for a sitrep.

It was surprisingly easy to find my Uncle Trifonas. I went to the local police station in Glyfada and they knew all about what had happened to us, as it was on the TV about this British military aircraft being forced into an emergency landing. One of the policemen could speak pretty good English.

FLASHBACKS

I explained my mother was Greek and I had family in Athens and I was trying to find them to say hello.

'Bravo,' he said, 'what are the names of your family?' I told him that my mother's family name was Kiousi, which was good because it wasn't like Smith.

'Kiousi is a name from the villages in the Peloponnese,' he told me. He went to check their filing cabinet and started rifling through the files. Then he stopped and said, 'I have found two Kiousis on record' – they had a criminal record for something but he didn't tell me. Instead he said, 'Ela tho,' which was 'come with me.' He took me in a Greek police car to a part of Athens called Kallithea. It was the home of my Uncle Trifonas. His name was like a God when my mother spoke about him. She would tell us such stories about the Germans he had killed with his bare hands.

When I arrived at the apartment, the policeman took me in and told the lady of the house that I was a British soldier off the plane that had been on the news. He told the lady my name was Michael and I was the son of Vasso kiousi and that he believed she must be my aunty.

The room was full of gorgeous women, who happened to be my first cousins. There was also a young boy, Kostas, who was the son of one of my cousins. I couldn't believe my luck or how happy I was at meeting my mother's family for the first time. They could not give me enough love, maybe it was because I was a boy and my uncle had nine daughters. My newly found aunty tried to phone my uncle, he was apparently getting drunk in some tavern.

As young Costas and a couple of my cousins could speak English we had a great afternoon, asking and answering

FLASHBACKS

questions about our family. My Aunty in the past would tell Trifonas a few lies to get him home from the Taverna, or he would drink and gamble and stay there all night. She finally got through to him and told him that I had arrived from England on the military plane that he had seen on the news that morning. He told her she had better not be lying or he would be angry. She told him it was true and sure enough a taxi pulled up outside and in walked this massive man, not tall but as broad as he was tall. He had not shaved for a week or so and at first I did feel slightly uncomfortable when he sat beside me on the settee and started to kiss me every few minutes. He asked about my mother, his beautiful sister. I lied of course saying that she was fine and she had a business and it was doing well. I don't think I fooled him, I believe he knew I was lying as he said if she was doing well why does she not come back to Greece to see him.

The truth was my Mother was battling to stay alive and deal with her own trauma, the trauma she had suffered, seeing her own family shot by the Germans.

I spent the next few days in and around Athens with my uncle and cousins. My uncle took me everywhere showing me off to his friends. The time that I remembered the most was when he took me down an alley just down from the Acropolis and stopped on the pavement. He then lifted up a trap door and we went down some steps into a cellar. We walked down the steps and immediately came face to face with about forty men sat around. There had been the noise of lots of people chatting and as we walked down the stairs into the cellar, the whole room suddenly went silent.

FLASHBACKS

My uncle put his arm around my shoulder and spoke to the crowd. 'This is Michael Kiousi, he is the son of my beloved sister Vasso.' He told them that I was a British soldier off the British military aircraft that had been forced to land in Athens. They all started clapping and cheering. He told me that they were all in the Resistance together with my mother and how they all loved my mother. A guy came over who spoke perfect English and said welcome to me. He translated what I told him to say to the people in the room. I said I was proud to meet all these resistance men, but the truth was that I was on my own, if they were thinking that I had come to rescue them. They laughed and started to tell me such wondrous things about my mother fighting the Germans. One even had a photo of my mother in British army battle dress. I was so proud of the mother, who in the past I had sometimes been embarrassed about, especially when she was in prison.

But that day in Athens was worth all the fear of the ordeal I had just been through getting to Greece. It was the day I found out why my mother was forever in pain and torment. Of course I told all of them how she was doing well and couldn't come to Greece because she had to take care of my younger brother and sister. I could see the sadness in the eyes of the men who had so much love for my mother. I made a promise to my uncle that I would one day bring his sister back to Greece. I didn't know when that would be as I was a British soldier and would be for the next many years, but I told them I would do it, if it was the last thing I did.

'Bravo,' he said. I did mean it, I told him, being in Greece that week, meeting all the family had filled me with so much

FLASHBACKS

love, as I never knew we had such a loving family.

My uncle explained that my mother married a British soldier and another sister, Mina, married an Italian soldier after the war.

I will come to understand more later on in my life, but at that time I was just so elated to have met my uncle and cousins. I gave them all the carvings I was bringing back from Kenya for my mother to sell. They replaced the space in my luggage made by the carvings with lots of Greek delicacies.

After six days of sheer happiness, we were told we were leaving and I was told to be at the hotel by twelve noon the next day.

I told my uncle that I was leaving in the morning. He told everyone he knew in Athens; all the resistance men I had met and all my cousins, some of whom had travelled a hundred miles just to see me. I knew the British fought at the side of many of these resistance men and it was as though those Greeks I had met in the Taverna were treating me as though we were back there in 1944.

I climbed into the back of the black Mercedes and sat at the side of my Uncle as we set off to the Hotel. As we arrived at the hotel, the rest of the guys were standing outside, awaiting the coach that would take us to the airport. They knew what a convoy was but they were shocked when I got out of the front of the black Mercedes in front of them. Then around fifty people got out of their cars behind me. They had all come to say goodbye to me. I once again promised my uncle that one day I would bring his sister home, as they all departed waving and tooting.

FLASHBACKS

My boss at the time, the Captain, asked me, 'Who are all those people Corporal Willey?'

I said, 'It's just the family.' It did look like something out of the Godfather, but I had never felt so proud to be Greek.

Once again I came back to the truth about my life at that time, a life that was now shrouded in confusion, sadness and despair. I didn't know what had happened to me to end up in the Woolwich Military Hospital, but I knew I needed to get better somehow. Both the nurse and John thought it must have been nice to meet all that family. I said I would have gladly crashed and died to get the feeling of love I felt for my mother and family after I had found out about her life. I did feel a little sad for John as like most soldiers that enlisted in those days, he came from the roughest part of town, like me, from a broken home and lacking in education. I would guess at least half of the servicemen joining the military in those days, came from broken homes or dysfunctional families.

I had listened to John for nearly six months, I had watched him and saw how he deteriorated mentally in front of my eyes, which is where he always was, or sat on the rugby pitch as I ran around.

He was there with his watch, sixty seconds Corporal,' it's as though his purpose in life was to time me running. Still I didn't mind as I had sort of took him under my wing and I was looking out for him whenever any of the other aggressive soldiers that were on the ward tried to attack him verbally, as John's favourite saying was, 'I am tired.'

That night after hearing my tale of woe, young john went off to bed and the corporal medic to his desk. The next morning the nurse came over and told us that we were all being given sick leave. We would be given our medication to take with us and we would be home for Christmas for two weeks. John turned to me and asked me if I was going on leave.

I said, 'Yes if they let me.' I had had another small operation on my face prior to going on leave so I was once again bandaged up, so I could go home and tell my family that I was in hospital for that reason. I would say anything in those days; I fell climbing or anything that stopped me having to explain what had happened to me, mainly because I didn't know what had happened to me.

By then I had been married and divorced and my ex-wife didn't want me in my daughter's life at the time, so home to me was to see my mother in Rotherham. The leave came around and I said goodbye to my mate John and the RAF Corporal who by that time had become like a prison guard that we had bought. He kept me informed about what was happening in the world and whether he was telling me so he could help me I never knew, suffice to say I trusted him.

I went home on leave with my face covered in plasters and I met a young girl on leave, her name was Carole, like me she came from a dysfunctional family and we fell in lust/love for a couple of weeks. At that time I wasn't a heavy drinker but, for some reason I drank myself stupid for two weeks and enjoyed my time with Carole. I tried to do the best for my mother, who by that time was struggling to keep afloat and as she was not getting any younger and having had six children, she was finding it hard to get a man who would pay for her attention. I gave her money all the time, but there was never enough.

FLASHBACKS

I went back to hospital after my leave, telling my mother I was stationed in London.

I arrived back on the Sunday night and managed to find an empty office in one of the wards and set about using the phone, as I always did with John. This time I was on the phone to Carole. I spent hours on the phone that night.

She said, 'It must cost you a fortune.'

I said, 'The army pays.' I hadn't told her what I was in hospital for, just that I had to have more treatment. The next day I just went for a run and chilled out, watched TV and waited for my mate to come back. John didn't return that day, so I asked the Matron, where he was. She was a Major in the Queen Alexandra Nursing Corps. She said she didn't know for sure but he may have gone back to his unit. I thought, no way.

I had his Grandmother's phone number as I had phoned it so many times for him I knew it off by heart. Before I rushed in I decided to wait and see the RAF Corporal Nurse who would be able to fill me in. Besides I couldn't get at a phone until the day shifts went off the wards. I found the Corporal and he looked at me in a strange way.

I said, 'Where is John Corporal?' He too came out with the bullshit.

He said, 'I believe he went back to his unit.'

I said, 'Two weeks ago John was not well and I knew he didn't want to go home as he asked me if I was staying.' I know his parents didn't give a shit about him, but his grandmother did as he spoke to her every other day. I told him I had John's grandmother's number and I was going to phone her that night. I also gave John the phone number of my friend in Rotherham if he got the chance to come over whilst on leave. That was

FLASHBACKS

when the medic told me the truth about the whereabouts of John. It was also the time that I found out what going back to your unit meant on that ward.

John had set off on leave, caught the tube to Kings Cross and got on the high speed train to Sheffield. He got as far as Loughborough before he pulled down the window in the door that was situated between carriages. People would stand there to have a smoke as at that time you could pull the window down quite far. The last person to see John was sat in the carriage next to the door who said she saw John leaning out looking out of the window. He suddenly climbed out of the window with his back to the outside and his bum sat on the window frame. The poor girl that witnessed it said, he appeared to be waiting. The witness said she heard a train hooter at the same time as she saw John just roll backwards into the path of the oncoming train on the other track. He did it so quickly no one had time to react.

I decided at that point that I was going to get myself better and fight again. I believed at the time that I owed it to John, my mother and daughter and all the family in Greece to live and try to forget about suicide. It wasn't to be my last time in the army that I would end up in hospital, but it was the beginning of the end of my army career. The next time I ended up in hospital was to be after my next fight as a soldier. I was medically discharged from the army for my physical injuries. That was to be the beginning of the real battle, the fight against my mental torture with suicide my constant companion.

Besides flashbacks, I now have nightmares to add to dreams. Shakespeare said, 'To sleep per chance to dream.'

FLASHBACKS

I say, 'To dream per chance to sleep.' The most common of my nightmares is the one where I see my young friend John with his handsome nineteen year old face smiling at me.

He is sat down with his back to the rugby posts as he times me running around the pitch, what starts as, sixty seconds Corporal,' with a smile from John on my first lap. By lap five, it has turned into a nightmare as every lap I run in my dream, turns Johns face and body into a mess. A look that can only come from a face and body that has been run over by a train or shot in the face. My mind imagines what his face and body would look like having been mangled under a train. As I have seen someone shot in the face that part of my mind brings the pictures to my dreams with ease.

As you can imagine, I am still ill from all those years of nightmares and flashbacks. But I will find my destiny and if I thought being a soldier was tough, my life after leaving the army was even tougher.

But I will find my destiny and come face to face with the person that saved my life. I cannot put what happens into words at this moment in time. I can sum up my life to press in three books: *'Angela's Ashes,'* for my childhood, *'A Bridge Too Far'* for my army career, and *'One Flew over the Cuckoo's Nest'* for the end of my army career.

The battle I will have as a civilian is like something out of *The Da Vinci Code*. I will identify who or what saved my life as a soldier and it will take me all my life to do that, but eventually the jigsaw of my life will be completed, between the flashbacks, or this book will be my epitaph.

Corporal Mick Willey

FLASHBACKS

Queen Elizabeth Hospital. Now a civilian hospital. Opened as Queen Elizabeth Military Hospital in 1972 and closed as a military hospital in 1995.

FLASHBACKS

Support the Best Armed Forces in the world

I have a friend in the Special Boat Service, the SBS are the marines equivalent of the SAS. I last saw my friend at the funeral of his father. His father being ex RAF and me being ex-Army we often got drunk together. We were good pals when Daniel was growing up and as such together we influenced Daniel to join the forces. At the funeral Daniel showed me a photo of himself receiving the Military Cross from Her Majesty The Queen at Windsor castle. He told me he had been on a patrol in Afghanistan and basically it resulted in a close quarter fight, with the Taliban, he told me they had killed the Taliban.

I have told you about my friend as he joined the marines, the same regiment as Sergeant Blackman. Daniel may not remember but he watched the film *The Guns of Navarone* with me and his father when he was around fifteen. In that film the patrol set out to destroy the German guns and along the way, they keep getting betrayed. It turned out that they had a woman in their company who was betraying them to the Germans. When they found out, David Niven who played the Corporal explosives expert tells everyone, she has to be shot. He does not care for that sort of thing as he has never killed anyone in cold blood. In the end, another Greek woman in the patrol shoots and kills the woman. As soldiers and marines we were brought up with such films and although I have never been in the same position as Sergeant Blackman. I believe he made the right decision as the leader of the patrol it was his responsibility to ensure the safety of the rest. The fact that he took the responsibility tells me two things about Sergeant Blackman.

FLASHBACKS

Firstly he is a very brave man as he had the courage to kill the enemy, even in cold blood. The second thing it tells me is that the courage came from the fact that he had already seen his comrades killed by the enemy. Having personally witnessed a soldier shot in the head by the IRA, who were the enemy at the time. I have no doubt in my mind that if I had the person who pulled the trigger to kill my friend in front of me, I would have done the same as Sergeant Blackman.

Yesterday I heard on the news about a poor American Special Forces Sergeant getting kicked out of the services for pushing an Afghan policeman to the ground. I also saw something about an appeal for our own marine Sergeant Alexander Blackman after he was jailed for killing an insurgent in Afghanistan. I am certain that Sergeant Blackman was suffering Post Traumatic Stress Disorder when he shot the insurgent. I went to bed at 11 p.m. last night with the thoughts of the injustice being dished out to the above two outstanding servicemen. I was awoken at 1.30 a.m. by my brother-in-arms who had been shot in the head in front of me in Belfast.

All I have on my mind is PTSD, PTSD, PTSD. I recover from that flashback, only for my mind to be taken on a night ride as I go from my friend being murdered to injustice after injustice. I keep going over the thoughts of injustice for our own Sargeant Blackman, constantly thinking it is all wrong. I look at the clock and it is 2.45 a.m. and I have been going over the same thing in my mind for over an hour.

I nod off again to be awoken at 4 a.m. by Corporal Derek Wood and Corporal David Howes, the two Signallers murdered by the IRA in the Northern Ireland graveyard in 1988. Why is no one fighting their corner, not only were they in the same corps as me, I knew them as I trained them as recruits. Watching them being publically brutalised then murdered was personal to me, like watching a brother murdered. Although I was not there at the time, I had done that same journey as them many times. I keep wondering why, we soldiers and servicemen have to pay the price twice for serving our country. The first price you accept, as it is your duty and you have been trained to serve queen and country. The second price should be paid by the country to the traumatised servicemen. The fact that our politicians would rather let a hero like Sergeant Alexander Blackman die a slow death in jail, mentally suffering as I know he is suffering, is a disgrace to our country.

I don't see the IRA coming forward and saying, by the way we found out the person who shot Paul Genge, another friend of mine from the army apprentice college. The IRA are not saying our man killed Paul in cold blood, so we have put him in prison. I don't see the Taliban coming on the TV and saying by the way we have put one of our own in jail for killing some British soldiers. It is only a British politician who could firstly kiss the backsides of the servicemen as he waves them off to war. Then it is only a British politician who would then put one of them in jail for doing his duty. Whatever the reason was for a soldier to kill the enemy, the fact remains they are the enemy. I have witnessed the behaviour of soldiers under fire and the results of the damage caused to the minds of soldiers. Having worked with many different nationality soldiers, I can confirm, what I was told when I enlisted. I was told the British army is the best in the world and I still believe that to this day.

FLASHBACKS

It is the best in the world because we have tradition, honour and men with courage who would lay down their life for Queen and Country. The Queen being the head of the armed forces has always led by example and shown her loyalty to her armed forces. In the same way all the Royal princes and Princess Anne have done in the past. Now Prince William and Prince Harry in particular have taken on that role. On Remembrance Day I spoke to Paul the ex Quarter master of the Blues and Royal. He told me how brilliant Prince William and Prince Harry were as officers.

It is that sort of conversations with servicemen and ex servicemen that makes the British Armed forces the best in the world, because our politicians may let us servicemen down all the time, but our leaders never do. I don't say these things because I have personally been helped by the support of the Queen and Prince William. The truth is I want our armed forces to remain the best in the world and to that end the government should not use our armed forces as a political tool. The government has done enough damage to our traditions in the armed forces, firstly dissolving famous regiments and now treating our own Sergeant Blackman like a criminal, is a crime in itself. I know through my own mental suffering that Sergeant Blackman and his family are suffering. As he suffers in jail every serviceman and ex serviceman in this country suffers. .

By their treatment, our own government is destroying the best armed forces in the world, by destroying the moral of the servicemen. We will always serve Queen and Country but if the government continue to destroy the moral of the armed forces we will not always win the wars.

FLASHBACKS

It is frightening enough when someone is shooting at you and wants to kill you, to put more fear in to the minds of soldiers when they go to fight for their country is totally wrong. If you want to put such pressures on people and then not support them when they come home traumatised, you go fight yourselves.

I joined the army at fifteen years old and Swore on my little black Bible to serve Queen and Country.

I did that for many years and was proud to do it, I am still here today, God didn't let me down, the Queen didn't let me down. The only people that let me down are the same people who let Sergeant Blackman down.

In the whole scheme of life and death, I am not an important man, I was just a British Army Corporal. Having said that Adolf Hitler was an Austrian Army Corporal responsible for my childhood having a distinct lack of grandparents and uncles on my mothers side. Being Greek my mother told me Prince Philip was our cousin. She never realised she was wrong, the truth is that he is a brother, a brother in arms as is Sergeant Blackman.

GOD SAVE THE QUEEN

FLASHBACKS

ROYALTY AND LOYALTY

A message for the government.

If you put a physically or mentally wounded soldier into a military hospital, with other military patients, looked after by military staff. The soldier will gain the strength both physically and mentally to recover and fight again.

If you send a wounded or traumatised soldier home to his real family and friends to recover, you condemn that serviceman and his family to years of mental suffering.

An injured soldier needs to be treated in a military environment, so he or she can have the mental banter that can only come from the minds of people who have served Queen and country. The Royal Family have always done their part and the government should do their part. The British government should take a leaf out of the American governments book.

American Military hospitals for serving servicemen (100 plus.)

American Military hospitals for veterans only (100 plus)

Greece Military hospitals (10)

Great Britain Military hospitals. (1 for Chelsea pensioners)
(1 for officers)

The fact remains that because we have no Military hospitals, we have no idea how many soldiers commit suicide due to service. Traumatised servicemen are discharged into the local NHS system and forgotten, only to be remembered by their friends and family when they drink themselves to death or commit suicide.